Love & Genetics

A true story of adoption, surrogacy, and the meaning of family.

by Mark MacDonald

and

Rachel Elliott

with original letters from Marilyn Elliott

For information contact: Unsolicited Press Portland, Oregon

www.unsolicitedpress.com orders@unsolicitedpress.com 619-354-8005

Cover Design: Kathryn Gerhardt
Editor: Kristen Marckmann

ISBN: 978-1-950730-90-2

Contents

Love &
Genetics

Prologue (Mark)

This was not the first time I had been in the Calgary airport, but it was the first time in years and my first time as an International arrival. My flight from Portland, Oregon had only taken ninety minutes and hardly seemed worthy of the designation "International," but the sign directing me to Customs and Immigration seemed stalwartly sure of it. My grey and tan North Face backpack was nearly empty. It had served me well since grad school and would continue to be my preferred carry-on for many years to come, but with just my laptop inside, it felt too light for air travel and refused to ride as comfortably over my shoulder as it should have. I had a checked bag too, but that was largely empty also—just a change of clothes, some toiletries, and a good bottle of wine that I hoped to share. I wouldn't be staying long, just the one night.

The morning plane touched down uneventfully and I was soon navigating the glass-walled maze of the international terminal. The myriad of signs and arrows were ostensibly guiding me toward customs, although the route clearly prioritized security over expediency. Fair enough. I readjusted my pack again, trying not to lose myself in thoughts of the day ahead. Through the glass I peered into the passing moments of other travelers—travelers already in Canada, travelers on the other side of the glass divide. I watched families trudge their way through the terminal with kids and bags straggling behind them. Lone adults passed time in a Tim Horton's with a cup of coffee and a MacLean's. Where were they headed on this Saturday morning? Where had they come from? Were they on time? Were they glad to be traveling? Were any of them worried about what they might find at their destination?

Airport customs was a small affair in Calgary; they must not get many international flights. There were only a half-dozen kiosks and only two of those were staffed by an agent that morning. But at 10:00 a.m. on a Saturday there was no need for any more. I paused at a high, narrow table near the back of the open room to scrounge through the second pocket of my backpack for a pen to fill out the blue and white customs form. Fortunately, I never cleaned my pack out completely, so there was always a pen, business card, or cough drop to be found in there when needed; I had, of course, double-checked for contraband before I left, knowing full well there wouldn't be any, but it's always worth being sure. My completed form in hand, I chose the kiosk on the left, the one with the woman agent and only one other traveler in line. After a rolling stop at the broad red line marked on the floor, I made my way to the side-counter of the kiosk, trying not to look nervous. It never helps to look nervous at a Customs and Immigration inspection. I reminded myself that I had nothing to hide here, I was not doing anything wrong. It was the rest of the day that I was nervous about.

The customs agent took my Canadian passport and opened it to the photo page. She looked me square in the eyes and then proceeded to size me up head-to-toe before returning her gaze to my hopefully anxiety-free face.

"Citizenship?" She began in a voice that was both friendly and tired, yet still held an undercurrent of authority.

"Canadian."

I had just handed her my passport, of course I was Canadian. I suppose they have to ask, perhaps to get a potential perjury on record, or perhaps just to see who they can trick. But it did say clearly right there on the front cover: CANADA PASSPORT (and then again in French, of course, PASSPORTE). It even goes a step further on the first page, explicitly listing my citizenship as CANADIAN, in case the reader had somehow missed the lettering on the outside cover. I imagined that once in a blue moon someone answers the citizenship question "Italian" while holding a passport from Albania and that's how they catch bad guys. The people who mess that one up must be extremely nervous-looking.

"Where do you live?" Her focus had now returned to her computer screen, which presumably listed all sorts of interesting details about my immigration credentials and prior travels.

"Portland, Oregon, in the States." I had been living in the US for more than a decade and had had this same conversation many times while crossing back into Canada at various borders. I had learned from experience that it did not serve to rush to any explanations or caveats, just answer their questions directly and succinctly and they'll get to the next part at their own pace.

"Why are you living in the USA?"

"I work for Intel Corporation there and live with my wife, who is American. I have a green card." I had my proof of residency at the ready and it was halfway across the side-counter before she asked for it.

"What are you doing in Canada today?"

This was the question I had been bracing for. Except for Tina, my wife, I hadn't told anyone why I was taking this trip: not my friends, not my job, not even my parents.

In that moment, my life as I knew it shrank from me and I felt utterly alone. But by law, here at the Immigration kiosk, I needed to be honest, and I had resolved to be plain about it. "I'm meeting my biological family," I said.

The agent paused and turned to look back up at me, ignoring her screen for a moment.

"First time?" she asked with genuine interest.

"Yes" was my spoken reply, although I was on the verge of tears and I'm sure that she could see that piece of my response as well.

"Well, you win the prize," she said with a wry smile. She stamped my passport and slid my documents back to me across the counter. "Best story of the day. Go on."

As I turned to head toward the baggage claim area, I heard her add "good luck."

"Thanks," I replied without turning back. I don't know if she heard me. I meant it, but I was too busy holding on to my edges to care about properly completing the social nicety. It was strange, surviving that one moment of honesty and the agent showing herself to be an ally of my quest. It allowed me to breathe normally again and gave me a tiny flush of confidence. Within minutes the world was slowly sinking back into the normalcy of airport navigation and I found myself successfully continuing to put my feet in front of each other as I made my way through baggage claim and on toward the rental car pickup. Searching for the right-numbered stall in the sparsely lit garage, I paused and felt the ground more solid beneath me than it had been in days. As I stood there, staring at the white Ford Focus in front of me, the customs agent's prize comment ran through my mind again, and it made me wonder.

Part 1 – Adoption

Chapter 1—In the Beginning (Mark)

It was late in the summer of 1999. I had just asked Tina to marry me and we lay in the dark of our tent listening to the steady thrum of rain drops beating on the nylon roof three feet above the tips of our noses. She had said yes, but between the rainy blackness of that night and our car being more than a day's hike away at the edge of the Adirondacks I'm not sure I gave her many other good options.

She turned to me in the darkness, her voice quiet and distant, "You know, with my kidneys..." I knew, as well as I knew there were tears in her eyes when she continued, "Are you sure?"

There aren't many moments in life when we are asked real questions, the kind of questions that seek to pry open the innermost doors of our hearts. I gave her question the space it deserved and peered into my own darkness to earnestly consider it before answering. The difficult truth was that I simply didn't know. Tina had kidney disease. She had lived with it since early childhood—permanent damage wrought by a severe infection and a fever that peaked at over 107 degrees. Amid the happiness of that moment in our tent, she felt compelled to remind me that her life might be different from that of other women. Her life span might be different. Things might get difficult for her and for me as her partner. These were legitimate concerns, even in the face of young love. But I hadn't come this far to turn around now, I loved her and was willing to take the chance. I don't make any decisions lightly, much less my decision to propose.

My response to Tina was trite, but I meant it. "We don't know what might happen to any of us. I might get hit by a bus tomorrow and end up paralyzed. Whatever happens, we can cross those bridges as they come. Together. Yes, I'm sure."

I turned on my pocket flashlight and aimed it at the third finger of Tina's left hand, which now bore a diminutive diamond ring, purchased on my paltry grad student salary. The tent lit up like a planetarium. The star-scape slid to and fro about our ceiling with the slightest movements of her slender hand. We had met four years prior at school at Cornell where we were both studying mechanical engineering. I spent my days playing with lasers in the lab and my evenings hanging out with friends—mostly her. What began as spending time together inevitably grew into something more. We became inseparable in a comfortable and reliable way. After three years of sharing each other's lives and apartments, we had come to know each other thoroughly. My proposal was little more than the natural next step in the progression of our relationship. I had no real doubts, and I hoped that she didn't either.

Nestled in our sleeping bags, we drifted off to sleep together looking forward to the weeks, months, and years ahead. And those times would indeed be mostly great for us—our wedding, graduations, career starts, and world travels together, not to mention the first-time novelty of disposable income. It was half a decade before we would come to our first impassible bridge.

We sat in uncomfortable comfortable chairs in front of a large wooden desk in a drab brown office on the outskirts of Boston. The brass and wood perpetual calendar on the desk read March 23, 2004. Framed degrees and shelves of leather-bound books adorned every square inch of wall-space. The doctor who we had met only twice sat across from us, a nephrologist who specialized in the management of high-risk pregnancies; he was accustomed to delivering unhappy news. This was not the first doctor we had visited to discuss the risks involved with Tina becoming pregnant, but it would be the last.

Test results and excerpts from medical journals were arrayed on the doctor's desk. The truth that we already knew now lay before us like an unsigned mortgage we couldn't afford, codified and undeniable. Tina would never be pregnant. Should never be pregnant. I understood the message. Technically, he explained, she could become pregnant, but her kidneys would never bear it. Even if she and the baby survived, it would mean dialysis and a dramatically shortened life expectancy.

The sound of the doctor's voice dwindled in my ears as he parsed the details, murmuring about numbers and percentages. He was speaking my own language of data and science, but even that could not pull my focus away from the internal dialogue that had started in my mind the moment I first scanned the pages of test results as he laid them out before us. I didn't need the details. I didn't need lists of contributing factors or tables from the various supporting studies. Comfort would not be found in lengthy explanations or consolations. It could only be found in finding a path forward. I'm lousy at accepting, it's simply not what I do. I calculate. I solve. I plan, and I try again. In my mind I had already let go of this defeat and had moved on to replanning my life.

We'll adopt. Adoption is good option.

I was adopted, and that worked out fine.

I was adopted.

To my surprise, the days that followed our meeting at the doctor's office led me on a path of reflection—not a journey I frequently undertake, except perhaps after a glass or two of single malt. It had been years since I had thought about my own adoption. It was at most a vague undertone in my life. I have always known I was adopted—I don't remember not knowing—but had rarely thought about it.

There were only two occasions in my entire childhood when I really thought about where I had come from. The first was a time when I was about eight years old and my adopted brother, Neil, was asking questions about his own biological roots. Neil is three years older and a very different person from me. He has not always made good choices. He is stubborn, sometimes tyrannical, and yet occasionally benevolent. Life has sometimes brought him to dark places, and he has not always emerged unscathed. Presumably those same troubles contributed to bringing questions about his adoption to the forefront for him at that age, but I don't know that for sure. After my parents had done their best to respond to Neil's questions, they asked me if I had any questions myself and I thought, why not?

My mother reached into the old yellow filing cabinet that lived in the corner of our breakfast nook and pulled out a small green card. The hand-printed card contained a few brief notes about my biological mother. Notes that had lain hidden within the unassuming quiet of that filing cabinet since the time of my birth, not five feet from where I ate my Cheerios every morning. The prospect of learning something about my biological roots immediately intrigued me, but the content of the card turned out to be perfunctory at best. She had been young, this woman with whom I shared my biology, only sixteen at the time of my birth. Beyond that, all I really got was long brown hair, medium build, and enjoyed tennis.

I had never really taken to tennis. I'm not sure what I expected to hear or how I expected to feel about the information on that small green card, but these few facts meant almost nothing to me. I went back upstairs to our third-floor kids' room to play and didn't think much more about that card for a quarter century.

The second occasion happened when I was in my early teens, just starting to become the person I was growing up to be. It was a typical cold and blustery winter day, and my mother and I were at the grocery store in the small underground mall at Yonge and St. Clair in Toronto. Underground stores are common in Canadian urban centers—in Toronto or Montreal one can shop, dine, and stroll for kilometers without ever being exposed to the harsh winter outside. As we were perusing the grocery aisles, accumulating the usual canned vegetables and cereals that were staples in our home, a woman I did not recognize stopped next to my mother.

"Liz! How have you been? I haven't seen you in years!" the woman gushed in the melodious tones of pseudo-sincere small talk that are common among people who only vaguely remember one another but are driven by social contract to speak anyway. "And this must be your son, Mark. He looks just like you!" My mother smiled at the woman and thanked her for the presumed compliment.

But I stopped short. *Wait, what?* Their conversation had moved on, but I was no longer listening, instead my easily galled teenage mind roiled. My response was visceral. An irrational rage welled up inside me, but it came from so deep inside that it couldn't quite make it to the surface and I merely stood there dumbstruck, turning the comparison over in my mind. I don't look like my mother. Her eyes are dark and mine are blue. Her hair is jet black and mine is light brown. Her nose has a completely different shape. Yet she seemed content to blur over those plain facts, not offering any corrections and, in the process, sweeping a part of me under the family rug. After a long couple of minutes, the conversation moved toward its inevitably polite conclusion as I stood there in stunned, silent shame.

Of course, I immediately rationalized the episode— calculating and solving as always. There was no reason to dig into the minutiae of my biological origins with a near-stranger in the vegetable aisle of this grocery store. My mother was just following normal social etiquette. Maybe she was even bothered by the remark herself? Maybe not. I never asked.

In truth, I have never had any real misgivings about my adoption. I had a good upbringing in a loving and supportive home. But physical resemblance, or lack thereof, has always been a sensitive topic for me. Never seeing the face of someone who looks like me—who was supposed to look like me—was deeply isolating. It wasn't sadness, nor was it merely curiosity. It was about belonging. The entire population of the world is an interconnected weave of biological identity. Most people can liken their physical appearance to their lineage across generations. Humanity's family tree is a roadmap that shows us how we are connected to each other, the world, and our history. As an adopted kid, I didn't know exactly where to find myself on that map. I understood, more or less, where my adopted family branched in, but it is a small comfort to know one's place on a borrowed path. For me, not knowing my biological roots—never seeing that face like mine—was about not knowing my physical connection to the world at large and, by extension, the true character of my own inner world. It wasn't tragic, but it was isolating. I was isolated.

Tina was in favor of us adopting a child—so many needy children in the world. She is the sort of person that always seeks to fix the problems of the world. She is a fervent recycler and a quiet defender of the downtrodden. She has devoted her career to energy conservation. Her zeal is founded less on the desire to be a caretaker, and more about her indignation toward inequity and her pragmatism about reducing waste. The idea of rescuing a child that needed a home fit comfortably within her paradigm. But she understood that my feelings on the subject were strong, if ill-defined. She gave me space to think, and largely let me drive our few discussions about the possibility of adopting children. Deference is not usually her style, but this was her loving me in her own particular way. We revisited the topic sporadically in the weeks and months that followed that fateful doctor's visit. There was no urgency. Time, if nothing else it seemed, was on our side—at least in the near term. We knew we had options and time to investigate them. Calculate. Solve. Plan. The way we'd always done things.

The first and most obvious option was domestic adoption. We soon learned that domestic adoption practices were rapidly evolving, and many new structures for adoption were being tried that did not exist when I was born. "Open adoptions," where the birth mother stayed in contact with the child and adoptive family, were becoming more commonplace, but they seemed to me to be fraught with risks. Open adoptions focus on supporting the child's sense of belonging, but perhaps at the emotional expense of the adoptive parents. Complicated families with complicated relationships.

There was also foreign adoption, but right from the outset, I knew I didn't want to adopt internationally. A racially distinct child carries the family's adoption as an external brand. Given my preoccupation with physical likeness, the notion of carrying such an external brand was terrifying to me. For the record, I'm not at all saying that international adoption is wrong, nor that adoption is ever a thing of shame, but for myself I wanted to at least have the chance to be mistaken as the true biological parent of my child. That irony was not lost on me, but neither was the desire mutable. International was not going to work for me. For us. Tina acquiesced on a foreign adoption without much resistance.

The truth was that any child Tina and I adopted, even one that shared our same racial ancestry, would almost definitely not look like me. I knew this and realized that building a family through adoption would not likely salve my sense of isolation. I would still lack that sense of belonging, only now across generations both forward and backward in time. A child without my features would serve as a constant reminder of that profound isolation. I couldn't cope with that. Eventually, it became clear that I simply did not want to adopt in any manner.

We changed gears and began considering some more radical options that might allow me the genetic progeny I seemed to be craving; surrogacy was one. Surrogacy could give me a child with a biological connection. But how? Who could we possibly trust with carrying our child? How would we find someone even willing? How could we ever ask that of someone? Where would we even begin? Every aspect of surrogacy seemed overwhelming.

The other option we gave serious thought to was sperm donation. Donation would be a path to continuing my genetic line—giving me, or at least my DNA, a semblance of a place in the world among future generations. But I would never know the child, I would lose the connection I was seeking before I even had it. And would I trust another, a stranger no less, no matter how worthy, to raise my precious offspring? While donation was possibly a solution, it was at least as fraught with dilemmas as the other options. Besides, I might be too shy to even enter such a clinic, much less to make a donation in one.

Calculate? Solve? Plan? The path forward remained unclear.

All these thoughts about different ways to build a family led me to seriously contemplate my biological roots and my place in the world. Strange feelings that had been kept buried deep within me for my entire life were finally being acknowledged. I wondered what happened to my biological mother after the sparse notes on that small green card were written down. I wondered about my biological father. But most of all, I wondered about the future of my biological line. I like to believe that I bring some value to the world in my own way and would prefer if my branch in humanity's family tree were not a dead end. A new and intriguing notion that I might have a half-brother or sister somewhere in the world made me tingle with excitement and curiosity. Would a half-sibling look like me? Would they act like me? Would they think like me? Not to mention that these hypothetical counterparts of myself might carry my genes (or at least a subset of them) into the future on my behalf.

These reflections and my discussions with Tina eventually bore two fruits. First, we would look seriously into gestational surrogacy as an option to have our own biological children together, despite the enormous challenges that surrounded it. In our early research, we found that there were services and law practices that could facilitate some aspects in most states, and we probably had the financial resources to make it possible, even if we weren't sure how to proceed. Second, I would begin a formal search for my own biological roots, starting with an attempt to find my birth mother. Perhaps if I saw her face, or knew something about her connection to the world, I would feel differently about adoption.

And so, there was a plan. Or at least the beginnings of one.

Chapter 2—Non-Identifying Information (Mark)

I was born, adopted, and raised in Canada. Like many societal things in Canada, adoption services are government administrated—in this case through the Children's Aid Society—so my quest for family roots began at a government information website. This one, like all government webpages, had an abundance of information and little actual guidance to offer, or at least little guidance of which I could make coherent sense. First, I had to download a small collection of forms and associated instructions. As I read through the instructions, I discovered additional requirements that didn't entirely make sense and would probably require different forms. So, I circled back to the homepage and looked again. It took only a couple of rounds of this before I gave up and started looking for a phone number. After deftly navigating the bilingual automated phone system (half in English, half in French—this is Canada after all) and waiting an appropriately lengthy time on hold, I finally got to talk with an actual person. At that point I was granted an unexpected reprieve: the voice behind this particular bureaucracy was genuine and kind. They were there to help me. They wanted to help me. An experience that was beginning to feel like doing my taxes was transformed back to something personal and manageable by the simple empathy in that one voice. This might only have been step one of many, but I no longer felt quite so alone in my quest.

During my initial contact with that voice at the Children's Aid Society, I was urged to submit "non-identifying information" about myself which they might someday share with a biological relative of mine, if one ever inquired. Non-identifying information, I was told, is a description of yourself and your interests intended to be shared without revealing your true identity or where you lived. Such information could be passed from biological child to parent or vice versa. I suppose that is all many adoption searchers are seeking—anonymous confirmation that an adopted child grew up to be a contented adult or relevant medical history details from a biological parent. Clearly this concept of non-identifying information had something to do with that inadequate small green notecard from so many years back. With that in mind, I agreed to the chore of writing something up, and resolved to myself to do a better job than the notecard did, regardless of whether anyone would ever read it.

I was surprised when the voice also told me that they had quite detailed non-identifying information from my biological mother that had been collected at the time of my birth—much more than a few bullet points on a notecard. Unfortunately, the wait to get that information sent to me would be about twelve months. Not the best-resourced agency in the government, I suppose. I agreed to fill out the paperwork to start that process as soon as possible and swallowed my sense of urgency as best I could. Requesting a search to locate a biological relative can only be done after non-identifying information is exchanged with the agency, and the wait for that service is an additional five to seven years. There were no other options.

So, there would be plenty of time. Too much time. More than enough time to think, doubt, regret, hold my breath, rethink, and hope. Already in my thirties, I reconciled myself to the understanding that age and biology might force our hand on the surrogacy versus adoption question long before I had a chance to complete a government-run search for my roots.

Nevertheless, I set out to write a description of myself. It is hard to describe how difficult that task was for me. I wanted to be honest and I wanted to be fair. But I also longed for approval from the reader(s) whom I had never even met. I couldn't decide if I wanted them to be proud of me, or regretful that they gave me up, or both, or neither. It was like composing a resume of my life—an awkward and conflicting process, a Battle Royale between my pride and my inherent shyness and my need for answers. I couldn't and wouldn't have finished it if it weren't a rigid requirement of the search process.

I sat motionless in front of a blinking cursor on a blank page for a long time before I could begin. And then I wrote and rewrote sentences in random order dozens of times. How can I summarize the story of my life in only a page or two? What aspect would be most meaningful or useful to a biological relative reading it? In the end, it was not so much a story as a list of white-washed self-observations, a peculiar mix of professional CV and online dating profile. Pride and the desire for approval from the ether seemed to have won out in the end, and it made me a little embarrassed to send in what I had written. I reminded myself more than once that I would probably be the only one to ever read it. More importantly, I reminded myself that the act of sending it in would complete that necessary first step in the lengthy search process.

Non-Identifying Information for Mark MacDonald, January 18, 2005

I have led a happy life. My adoptive family has always been loving and supportive. I have one elder brother (adopted also) who is 3 years older than myself. I have not always gotten along with my brother (we are different people), but we are reconciling as we get older. My grandparents have all passed now. I liked them but we were never close as they lived a long distance away (England and Vancouver).

I am a little more than 6 ft 1 in and roughly 190 lbs. I was very slim (<160 lbs.) until I reached the age of 28. I have blue eyes and dark brown hair. I was blond as a young child and then my hair slowly grew darker each year until I was about 16. I have red facial hair (for the past eight years I have worn a goatee). I am athletic and enjoy soccer, basketball, and skiing. When I was in high school, I also did a lot of middle- and long-distance running.

I am happily married to a woman who is half Finnish, half Sri Lankan, and who was born and raised in Alaska. We have no children at this time but are thinking of adopting. I have always loved animals and we have several pets (three cats and one dog). I have had cats as pets for nearly my entirely life. We own our own home and live comfortably.

I am quite smart and well educated. My adoptive family has always provided for every opportunity. I have always done exceedingly well in school (although not always applying myself as much as I should have). I graduated near the top of my class from Queen's University in engineering and earned a Ph.D. from Cornell University. Throughout university I was always the one that people would come to when they needed help. I am now a licensed mechanical engineer, specializing in the investigation of fires and explosions. I have a good job as an engineering consultant working in the USA, although at some point I hope to return to university as a professor.

I have a fairly good sense of humor (although it is generally sarcastic in tone), and I even drew cartoons for a campus newspaper in college. My first published cartoon was a picture of Superman with his head embedded in a large bullseye and a caption that read "Faster than a speeding bullet, but less practical for target practice."

I tend to have a few close friends rather than many acquaintances, although in recent years my Christmas card list seems to be growing longer and longer. I usually prefer a quiet night at home watching a movie over going out on the town. I like to read but do so slowly. I enjoy the outdoors (canoeing and hiking) and camping. I spent eleven years in Boy Scouts growing up, eventually earning the Chief Scout Award (a.k.a. the Queen Scout Award). I have traveled to Europe (Germany, England, Italy, and Holland), Japan, Jamaica, and Brazil.

I am not a religious person, in the sense of organized religion, but also not a complete atheist. I have fairly liberal political beliefs and am a staunch environmentalist (I drive a hybrid electric vehicle).

I have led a relatively healthy life. I have had numerous injuries from all my sporting activities (broken bones, one torn Achilles). I have had seasonal and household allergies since puberty.

I have never been able to competently play a musical instrument but have a keen ear (a former music teacher told me I had perfect pitch). I have done some amateur photography. My work was always more interesting than good.

As soon as it was done, or at least done enough, I mailed my non-identifying information to the Children's

Aid Society, expecting nothing and also expecting everything, and then the waiting started. This wait would be far too long for me to allow myself to look forward to a response. It was not delivery in six-to-eight weeks, it was a full year of my life. I had no interest in losing an entire year to the tyranny of rapt anticipation, especially when the culmination would not be final answers, but merely the beginning of the next step in the search process. So, I bottled up my emotions and did my best to go on with my life as it was. Of course, curiosity lingers, whether you want it to or not.

A little less than a year later, I received a thin package from the Children's Aid Society. It came by regular mail on an unremarkable day in an unremarkable oversized envelope. I knew what it was as soon as I saw the return address in the upper left corner. Children's Aid Society, 30 Isabella Street, Toronto, Ontario. Inside was a white card-stock folder with blue lettering and a collage of pictures of happy children printed on the cover. I opened the folder to find a number of sets of stapled pages and color brochures. There were instructions and supporting materials, and most importantly, five glorious typewritten pages of non-identifying information about my biological mother. My hands were shaking more than usual as I took these pages out. One day soon I would learn that my shaky hands are a genetic trait that runs in the family.

A handwritten note on the cover page read: *The following information was taken from the files of the Children's Aid Society of Metropolitan Toronto and includes all non-identifying information available.* Curiously, the document was dated October 1985, fully twenty years prior to my request, but also twelve years after my birth and adoption. I'm still not sure what to make of that timing, except that it reinforces my suspicions about government bureaucracy. It was later semi-explained to me that the document was a summary of notes taken by a nurse who had attended to my biological mother at the time of my birth, later compiled and written up by a social worker who removed any identifying information from the notes.

I forced myself to sit down at the mission-style oak desk in our home office and took a deep breath. Then I turned over the cover page and began to read:

Non-Identifying Information from my biological mother, October 4, 1985

Background History for Mark Angus MacDonald

Mark was born at 10:43 a.m. at Scarborough General Hospital on January 4, 1973. He weighed 9 lbs., 11 oz, after a 43-week term. His Apgar was 6 at 1 minute, 9 at 5 minutes. He was admitted to care and placed in a foster home until placed on adoption February 19, 1973.

Mark's mother was born in Alberta in 1956. She was 5'6" with an average build, reddish-gold blonde hair, brown eyes, and fair skin. She was described as a pretty, vivacious looking girl with an oval face. She had very large feet.

She was an intelligent girl who was mature at times but also very much an adolescent who could be giddy and impatient. She had an enthusiastic attitude toward life, lots of friends, and a resourcefulness and thoughtful approach to problems.

She had completed Grade 11 and left school in Grade 12 due to pregnancy. She was continuing some courses through correspondence. English was her favorite subject and she also enjoyed biology. She did not like math or physics.

She was interested in art which she had studied in high school and liked to do portraits in pencil or charcoal. She also enjoyed individual sports, was a cheerleader and in the drama club.

She grew up in the Mennonite Church and was active in the Young People's Organization. Both physical and mental health were good.

The birth mother's father was about 46 years old and about 5'4" with a stocky build, dark honey hair, blue eyes, and a large prominent nose. His health was good and he had always worn glasses for farsightedness. He had attended Bible college and worked as a farmer. He was described as quiet, easily hurt, and not a person who spoke out. He was a good cook and played the violin. A very religious person, he was involved in his church and taught Sunday School.

Her mother was 47, 5'5" with a stout build, and dark-brown straight hair. She was a nice-looking woman said to be German in appearance with high cheekbones. She completed Bible college and was described as the financial manager and mainstay of the family. She was the parent who disciplined the children. Her health was good and she too had "huge feet."

There was a 21-year-old brother, 5'7" with a muscular build, dark-brown straight hair and blue eyes. He did weightlifting, was athletic and completed a course in computer programming.

A sister, 18, had dark brown hair and eyes. She was 5'3" and 115 lbs. with large bone structure. She completed Grade 12 and was studying to be an RNA. She was described as quiet and religious, interested in cooking, sewing, and nature.

The younger brother was 14 and not yet 5'. He was slender with a muscular build, whitish blonde hair and a "huge nose." He had a brain tumor that required surgery, missed two months of school and still obtained a 90% in Grade 11. The birth mother described him as a genius who planned to become a scientist. He played piano, violin, and accordion by ear.

The younger sister was 13, a cute blonde with blue eyes who was expected to be tall. She had difficulty concentrating in school and had repeated one year. She also had some difficulty making friends.

Paternal grandfather was of Scottish descent, about 70 years and in reasonable health. He had been a car salesman and was described as a comedian and hilarious. He played mouth organ by ear. Grandmother was also Scottish and about the same age. Her interests were domestic.

Maternal grandparents were of German descent and described as a typical farming family, now retired. Grandfather played the fiddle by ear and grandmother made excellent doughnuts.

There was one paternal aunt in good health and 8 or 9 maternal aunts and uncles. All were in good health. The women were described as big and the men handsome. The family was musical and several played piano or violin.

Mark's birth father was born in Ontario in 1951. He was 6' with a slender build, small triangular face, well defined nose and mouth. He had a mass of frizzy, curly brown hair. He dressed casually, but had a neat, clean appearance.

He was described as an outgoing person with a lot of friends and as being fun at a party. He could express himself clearly, was ambitious to be an entertainer, and was good at ad-libbing and acting as Master of Ceremonies.

He completed Grade 13 and was accepted at both a university and a college but was not able to go immediately because of finances. He hoped to be able to go in the future as he wanted to teach.

He was an athletic young man involved in track, football, and hockey. He was a particularly good runner who participated in some major track meets. His health was good.

He had worked as a day laborer and at the time of Mark's birth was in a manager trainee course in a retail business.

His parents attended a fundamentalist church, but he was no longer affiliated with any religion.

The birth father's father was in his 40's and of Anglo-Saxon origin. He was 5'11' with a heavier build than his son and reddish, light brown hair. He was in good health and never missed work. His father left the family when he was 6 years old so he worked from an early age. He completed Grade 13, wished to go to university but took up carpentry instead. He too was athletic and excelled in running. He was highly intelligent and had a collection of old books, some of which were confiscated and burned by the R.C.M.P. during the "Red Purge." He was active in his church and attended regularly.

His mother was as tall as her husband and had a large frame. She was working part-time as a receptionist. She was not active in the church nor was she particularly domestic. Her husband and sons did most of the cooking. She was adopted in Scotland at age 4, and the family then moved to England and Canada. She had made enquiries about her birth family and understood that the father was the son of a nobleman and the mother the "upstairs maid." Her birth father was said to be related to Bonnie Prince Charlie.

The birth father's oldest brother was 24, shorter but more muscular and completing law school. He was on the Dean's Honor List. He was healthy and also athletic.

A sister, 23, was tall with a big frame and reddish hair. She completed Grade 13 and worked as a lab technician.

31

The younger brother was 15, 6' with a big frame and curly brown hair. He was in Grade 11, quiet, good looking, and a football player. He attended church and was the family cook.

The younger sister was 13 and becoming tall and slim. She was in Grade 7 or 8 and the birth mother described her as spoiled.

Parental grandparents were Anglo-Saxon and both died in their 80s. Maternal grandparents (adoptive) were also deceased. There were 3 or 4 paternal aunts and uncles, all tall and athletic.

The birth mother grew up in a close, strongly religious family. She was the outgoing member and was rebelling against some of the restrictions. At the same time, she was very attached to them.

The birth parents met playing tennis 3 years earlier and at first couldn't stand each other. The relationship grew to be meaningful, although her parents did not approve because the birth father was not of their religion. The pregnancy came as a shock to the birth parents, and they decided early that adoption was the best plan as they were not ready to be parents.

They were supported in this by both families. The birth mother came to Toronto and entered a Maternity home until Mark was born. She was very proud of him and thought he was a beautiful baby.

It appeared that the relationship would continue and the birth mother's family became more accepting of it. However, neither of these young people were ready to make a commitment to marriage at that stage.

It was strange to read, and somehow discordant with what I recalled from the green card. It felt disappointingly bland and uninsightful, almost intentionally impersonal.

My hopes receded rapidly as I read. When I finished, I felt unfulfilled. I'm not sure what I had expected to read. I scanned my eyes up and down over the pages, rereading portions of what I had already read more than once, searching for something more. While grateful for these haphazard nuggets, I still felt slighted by a government process that was inefficient and imprecise in its ability to document what was for me monumentally important information. In the world of science and engineering, my world, critical analysis and thorough documentation are essential skills. I suppose I was not entirely used to finding them so lacking. Regrounding, I reminded myself about beggars and choosers and decided to focus on moving forward.

The white and blue folder also contained the forms to formally request a biological relative search. I withdrew them, closed the folder, and set about completing them right away. I mailed out the request the next morning, thus beginning the search for the large-footed woman who bore me, and then I returned to waiting—long, lonely, merciless waiting.

I am compelled, not entirely of my own choosing, to note that years later when I finally had the opportunity to meet my birth mother in person, her feet were revealed to be of perfectly normal size. She was much chagrined that anyone would have the nerve to imply otherwise.

Chapter 3—An Ordinary Life (Rachel)

I may be wrong about this, but I'm pretty sure no one wants to admit to being ordinary. We each spend our lives, in varying degrees, trying to find The Thing that makes us unique, The Thing that makes us stand out from the masses, The Thing that makes us each a special snowflake. The very idea of saying, out loud, that I am an ordinary girl actually pains me. But there it is. I feel like I need to be upfront about this, right from the start. While my mother will tell anyone within earshot that I am special, it seems necessary to qualify that it is in a very regular and commonplace way.

I'm a pretty girl but was never singled out as a striking beauty. I'm smart, too, but as long as we're being honest, I'm no genius. I'm friendly but was never the popular girl. I led a scandal-free life as a teen and married young for love. I had my daughters while in my early twenties—planned and prepared for, just like the books suggest, with the appropriate number of receiving blankets, ergonomic bottles, rectal thermometers, and an inordinate number of diapers. Meanwhile, like the rest of the people I knew, I struggled to find a way to be myself, to let my little light shine.

It's easier to shine when we're little, I think. Spunky, brown-haired eight-year-olds can ride their bikes through the neighborhood, pigtails flying, wearing a Wonder Woman bathing suit two sizes too small, and the adults smile indulgently. When they climb trees in their Sunday best and rip their tights, no one gets exasperated but their mothers. There is always something to pull us from the reality of life when we're young; always an imaginary land to be explored or daring adventure to be had. It seems to me that Ordinary somehow creeps in along the way when we're not looking. While studying for midterms or filling out college applications it slips along the floor under the bottom of the bed, and gradually wraps itself around our feet while we sleep, until taking a step that isn't in line with all the other steps starts to feel too risky and eventually becomes almost impossible. We wake up one day and suddenly, it seems, there is no way we could put on that Wonder Woman bathing suit again.

Despite the creep of Ordinary, the idea of carefully following the path has always chafed me. So, one day on a whim I got a toe ring at a kiosk in the mall and enjoyed the feel of it like a secret rebellion in my shoe. A year later I got a nose ring, which my husband professed to love. I mourned when it fell down the furnace vent and was lost forever. Then I got a tattoo after winning a brief but furious marital skirmish, and finally began to feel like I was standing out among the crowd of young moms I found myself in. And that's about it, I have to admit: a toe ring, a nose ring down the vent, and a palm tree with hearts on either side (one for each of my daughters). I have not lived a spectacular and daring life. I'm an ordinary girl, in an average home with a loving husband and happy daughters. We are just a normal family. You could say my home is nothing to write home about.

Please don't get me wrong because I'm not complaining. I'm just trying to give a sense of context. It's important to know where I'm coming from, because when the ordinary is about to become extraordinary, it's difficult enough to explain what a shock it is to suddenly find oneself in a completely unordinary life.

"I love you."

"It's cancer."

"I'm pregnant."

"It's over."

The words that undo us are strung together so simply. It's rarely the long conversation that turns our world upside down, leaving cracks in our life like asphalt in the winter, just small words in simple forms. It was four such words that changed everything ordinary for me.

I had reached a point in my life where the past was a known quantity. Stories of family history had been unraveled over the years, old knots untangled with each maturity milestone. Through the telling and retelling, these tales slowly reconciled themselves to the parents I thought knew, and I assumed the rest of my surprises would be born from the horizon, out of the mysterious, far-off future. So, when I sat down across from my mom in Chili's on a cold Calgary night, I had no idea what I was in for. It was because of this I was barely paying attention when she began:

"I had a son."

I popped another awesome blossom peel into my mouth. No big surprise there. "Two, actually," I murmured around the hot, greasy onion.

"Three, actually." There was a long pause. "Another son. Before I was married."

I was six months pregnant with my second child, another girl. Somehow, it was this momentous occasion, not the birth of my firstborn that brought on her out-of-the-blue confession. We were sitting at a table for two in the back on a crowded weeknight dinner service, and I found myself suddenly busy making sure my coaster was centered in the bright ceramic tile of the table. I was desperately wishing for a margarita that would never come, as only a pregnant woman can, when she reasoned, "Now that you are having your second child, I think you are old enough to hear this." How random is that? What was it, exactly, that being pregnant a second time did to qualify me for this?

Her words, *Before I was married,* echoed almost without meaning in my head. This, from her, was dumbfounding. I was raised in a home where abstinence before marriage was a seriously held belief, among numerous others, so this was the last confession I expected to hear. I had no context in which to understand it. But there it was, lying between us on the table. Four simple words. Suddenly the past blindsided me. What? Everything that was known became a little bit . . . unknown. A tsunami tossed my memories head over heels. All my childhood assumptions and experiences were cast in a different light.

It was like the time she picked me up after school in the ninth grade and, stopped by the red light, turned around with sudden, urgent tears and said, "You know that if you ever got pregnant you could come to me and I would help you—we would find a way."

What?

How did we get from math homework to teen pregnancy?

Ohhhhh. Now I see. My Secret Brother, that's how.

I was immediately consumed. I wanted to know every scrap of information, every detail she knew. She began telling me about seeing my dad, a senior, walk across the tennis court in his white shorts. He was the big-man-on-campus, a jock with a trail of girls wherever he went. She was smitten. With her wide smile and brown eyes, it wasn't long before he noticed her, and their relationship began with the tiny lie of her age. Adding a year was enough to nudge her out of childish and into dateable. It wasn't long before the two were inseparable.

The server came by to see if we needed anything, but the hushed, urgent tones of my mom's voice and my own shocked, tear stained face were enough to keep her from interrupting. I noticed the couple across the aisle look at us with concern, but other than those two small moments, the world had emptied to just me, mom, and her story.

Young love turned to teen pregnancy. I couldn't help but do the math in my head.

My grandpa, a man I only knew to be quiet and benign, had pushed for her to abort the baby, but she is not now, and was not then, a person who is easily cowed. She refused, and her parents ended up pulling her from school and sending her to a home for unwed mothers in Toronto. My dad only visited a couple of times. I couldn't really tell from her story whether they were still dating at this point, but I do know she named her firstborn son after him—Stephen. A name that would be etched into her heart, but never go on a birth certificate.

Their son was given up for adoption. My mother went home, and no one in her family ever spoke of it again. Ever. My parents continued dating after that as though nothing had happened. She told me, weeping into her napkin, that she and dad had never even talked about him, even after their wedding two years later. The son that was born became a secret she held alone.

As she spoke, I listened in stunned silence, tears rolling down my face into my uneaten quesadilla. I was bursting with questions, but she had precious little to tell me about him, other than he existed. Her words came as an apology, but to me they were an astonishing revelation. Until that moment, I had been the oldest in my family. But now there was a mysterious Secret Brother, a full-blooded brother, who I had never known about! She swore me to secrecy, telling me that my two younger brothers didn't know, and dad didn't even know that she was telling me.

That night, the idea of my Big Brother was planted in my mind like a secret garden, a place I visited alone to wonder who he was, where he was, and what he was doing right at this very moment. Were we in the same time zone? Was the sun setting on him too, or as I got ready for bed, was he drinking his morning coffee? Did he even drink coffee? I spent that night, and many after it, imagining his life and wishing I knew him. It took a long time before I was willing to admit to myself that knowing he existed would probably have to be enough; that I would never know the man my long-lost brother grew up to be.

Chapter 4—Searching for a Unicorn (Mark)

Surrogacy is hard. Actually, surrogacy is expensive; finding a surrogate is hard. And not "finding a good dentist" hard, it's more like "finding your dream job" hard—and I'm not talking about merely a good job, but truly a *dream* job, you know, the one where they pay you exorbitant sums of money to sleep late and while away your afternoons sharing your wisdom in the intellectual salons of Paris over many glasses of fine Bordeaux. Just like willing and healthy surrogates, we believe that such dream jobs exist, because we hear about them every now and then, but how you end up with one is a complete mystery, seemingly ruled more by the fates than any action or talent of your own.

Frankly, why should it be easy to find a surrogate? Extraordinary sacrifices are asked of them—who would sign up for such a role? What women would risk her very life to carry a child in her womb that was not hers and would never be hers? And it's not just the pregnancy, birthing, and months of physical recovery, but also giving up alcohol, caffeine, cigarettes, hair dye, and the litany of other indulgences that are off limits to the expecting? It seemed too much to ask of anyone. Even assuming we could find a willing surrogate, and at the time that felt less likely than finding a unicorn, could I bring myself to trust someone other than Tina to carry our unborn infant child? The prospect of surrogacy was intellectually attractive, but the reality of it was beyond reason.

Every state has its own laws regarding surrogacy. Some states forbid any sort of financial support from the would-be parents, presumably for fear of creating a distasteful *rent-a-womb* perception. But medical bills are real, as are the challenges of working while pregnant, so other states allow parents to cover medical expenses for a surrogate and even provide a stipend for them to live off.

In Massachusetts, where Tina and I lived at the time, it was illegal to compensate a woman for serving as a surrogate for you. The aforementioned unicorn would need to be acting solely out of the goodness of her heart. That pretty much limits one's options to siblings or an extraordinarily close friend. My brother Neil was obviously not a candidate. Even if he were the right gender, self-sacrifice and responsibility are not often counted among his virtues. Tina has a sister, Anita, but she was a few years older than us and already outside the target age window for a prospective surrogate. After careful thought and calculation, we screwed our courage to its sticking place and approached one of Tina's oldest and dearest friends, a single mom in her own right. We should have known it was far too much to ask, with the economic implications and personal risks, our proposition didn't merit even passing consideration on her part, no matter how earnest her hopes were for us. Upon reflection, it was probably not even fair of us to even approach her, but the clock was ticking and our options were limited. It was a quick defeat for us, in what had already been a dishearteningly long series of defeats.

While I was not yet ready to give up entirely, the idea of surrogacy that had started as a legitimate possibility in my mind was quickly diminishing into mere fantasy under the heady weight of reality. Our calculations on this effort weren't holding up. The math was wrong.

In the summer of 2005, I was offered an interesting job opportunity with Intel Corporation in Oregon. They wanted me to help them develop a technology pathfinding capability for notebook cooling. Essentially, I would help them find new and better ways to stop notebooks from getting too hot on your lap. At the time, both Tina and I were ambivalent about our current jobs in Massachusetts—I was straining under the stress and workload of my position, and Tina was thirsting to apply her thermal sciences knowledge to something more impactful to the planet; at the time she was working in fire safety, which was worthy but unfulfilling for her. Oregon, being a well-known hotbed for alternative energy initiatives, seemed like a natural fit for us, career-wise, so we took the plunge (even without a job lined up for Tina) and relocated to the Portland metro area in early 2006.

Moving to Oregon was good for us. It did not take long for Tina to find a job in energy consulting that both challenged and rewarded her. Meanwhile, I settled in quickly at Intel. Electronics cooling was adjacent to my background of expertise and I enjoyed the challenge of digging into new areas like computer system design, thermal ergonomics, and aeroacoustics. Outside of work, the two of us embraced the many pleasures of living on the West Coast: fine wines, outdoor recreation, warm and welcoming neighbors, and a rugged coastline that runs forever. We also found some unexpected help on the surrogacy front—Oregon law, unlike Massachusetts, allowed for compensation and health care support to be paid to a gestational surrogate. As a result, surrogacy in Oregon was more common than in many places in the US. It was certainly not prevalent, but people seemed to consider it merely unorthodox and not completely mad. This change in attitudes reinvigorated the idea of surrogacy for us and within a couple of months of our move, we met with an attorney who specialized in surrogacy cases and began researching the regional surrogacy services online with faint hopes of finding our unicorn.

One aspect that we hadn't fully appreciated yet was the true scale of the finances involved. Being only a few years out of graduate school, the numbers were daunting. Locating a willing surrogate might be possible here, but we would need to save some serious money first. With both of us now working good jobs, and cost of living in Oregon being significantly less than it was in Massachusetts, it did not seem completely impossible, but we would definitely need to save. In addition to the cost of healthcare for the surrogate, there was the compensation, on the order of $35,000, agency and legal fees galore, and, of course, the substantial *In Vitro* Fertilization (IVF) costs. For a surrogate to carry our future child, we would need the help of many doctors and specialists to harvest viable eggs from Tina, fertilize them with my sperm, and surgically implant them in her. Surrogacy is a lot more than the turkey-baster/specimen cup exercise that some people imagine it to be. There were many required hormones, medicines, clinic facilities, and doctor bills that would need to be paid, and none of it would be covered by our health insurance. All told, the full cost would be something like $100,000 in after-tax dollars. That's about four and a half brand-new reasonably equipped Toyota Corollas and not the kind of money we had just lying around.

The shifting barriers being placed in front of the surrogacy option were continuing to seem insurmountable. A pragmatic question surfaced: could the biological connection I was seeking possibly be worth that kind of investment, an investment largely for me that

Tina and I would both have to sacrifice for? Between the legal, financial, social, and medical complications, it began to feel like it would just be easier to walk away, live a normal life, and just cope with my lingering questions as best as I could. People lead ordinary lives all the time. Everybody has issues with which they struggle. And there are plenty of folks in my exact situation—absent of any biological relatives in their lives—and they all seemed to survive just fine. I had already made it through my first thirty-five years; the ordinary life was well-trodden territory for me.

I reminded myself that there was still a chance that my search for my biological mother might bear fruit. Perhaps the surrogacy part of the dream was not meant to be, but I might still find solace in the reconnection part of the dream. Not all dreams come true.

Chapter 5—In Confidence (Rachel)

My baby brother and I were driving to pick up pizza over Thanksgiving weekend in the fall of 2006. There are only so many times you can eat turkey in a two-day period before you just need something that's not turkey. When I got married in 1994, Vincent was only twelve, and so although we are brother and sister, I didn't know him, not really, until he was an adult. Since then, much to my delight, he's become one of my best friends. A tall and handsome boy, he is brash and funny and gentle all at the same time. He was studying at the University of Kentucky at the time, majoring in the major of the week, dating the girl of the week, and living above my parent's garage—which is why clichés are true. While we drove into town to get the pizza, we were lamenting the way our parents' relationship had devolved into what seemed like one long bicker. Mom and Dad were becoming Mom versus Dad, at least a little. Truthfully, what had driven us from the house, even more than the turkey, was the *Battle of the Snap*.

Dad, Vincent, Curtis, and I had been playing poker over taco chips and wine. I innocently noted, while lamenting my diminishing pile of nickels, that Dad snapped his cards down with a certain smug vigor as he displayed his winning hand, one card at time: snap snap snap snap snap full house. My comment was met with raucous agreement from The Boys, and as the conversation escalated in both volume and wine-driven silliness, a voice rose up from the other side of the room.

"I hate it when your father snaps cards. It reminds me of when we were young."

One long bicker.

Growing up we had largely experienced our parents as a team, a couple who loved each other steadily through the years of raising a family while Dad preached on Sundays and mom managed a one-income household with never ending resourcefulness. So as the silliness turned serious, and card snapping brought up long-dead topics like gambling debts we'd never heard of, we all grew unsettled. There were things we didn't know about.

"Shit, it's good to get out of the house," he sighed as we turned out of the driveway, probably a little too full of wine to be driving. "Mom and Dad are making me crazy."

Cautiously, into the dark, I said, "I know. She pushes his buttons all the time."

We made it to the top of the hill before I chanced, "I think they've got things they need to talk about, you know?"

"No shit." Pause, signal, right-hand turn. "What do you mean?"

"Nothing, nothing." Hastily, I tried to backpedal. "Just that you can't be married for thirty years and not have things to work through, that's all." Pause. "Why? What did you think I meant?"

He just shifted in his seat, adjusting the rear-view mirror as we cruised along Jessamine Station Road.

"What do you know, Vincent?"

"Why? What do you know, Rachel?"

The car fell meaningfully silent. I leaned forward in my seat, unable to keep the words from tumbling out of my mouth. "Can you keep a secret?"

"Who would I tell?"

"No, really. You have to swear to me that you will . . ." I was about to make him promise his first-born child when he stopped the car short of the beckoning neon of Little Caesar's and looked me quizzically in the eye under the glow of the parking lot lights.

"Is this about our Secret Brother?"

I have always been thought of as the keeper of the family secrets. Vincent would be much more apt to blab. He must have assumed I knew.

It had been six years since the first revelation from my mother, and now I was sitting in the front seat of my baby brother's 1991 Honda piece-of-shit in the parking lot of Little Caesar's, home of the Hot 'n Ready, finding out that he knew! My world shifted again. I was stunned.

"Yes! I'm talking about our Secret Brother!" I yelped at him. "What the hell? You know?"

Vincent was disappointingly matter of fact, possibly already thinking about pizza. "Mom told me a couple of years ago, when I was moping about being the black sheep of the family, about blah blah blah I have so many flaws and fuck-ups. She was like, 'You think you're the black sheep in this family? You have no idea.'" He grinned at me widely. "So, she told me that her and Steve had a baby before they were married. We have a Secret Brother! Cool, right?" This is how conversations go with Vincent. But he was right. It was cool.

The drive home was too short. The hot pizza burned my lap through my jeans and we wondered back and forth where he was, what he was like, who he was. With only three minutes or so to speculate, we arrived at the conclusion that no matter what, he was probably a spectacular human being, much like ourselves. Intelligent, handsome, charming, and funny, definitely. Our conversation bounced around the car like helium balloons, inflated with the sheer happiness of the idea of him. We sat in the car in the driveway outside our parent's house, my burning lap notwithstanding, and agreed that we wanted to find him. I told Vincent that I had looked into it.

"I wrote a letter to Oprah," I confessed.

He barked out a laugh. "You dummy. Are you kidding me? Did you get anything back?"

I shrugged. "Naw, just a form letter response. I started trying to look online but it's so much more complicated than I thought it would be. I surrendered."

Our conversation was halted by the front door opening. Dad called out, "What's going on out there? Bring in the pizza already, would you?"

For the rest of the night, our Secret Brother was like the silk thread of a spider's web between Vincent and me. He would catch my eye and raise an eyebrow like he does, or smirk knowingly, and I knew he was thinking about this older brother we had never known. Before that night and our short, honest trip to Little Caesar's, I sometimes wondered if I'd imagined the whole conversation with my mom—she never mentioned it to me again after that first time. Over the years, the reality of my Secret Brother had faded into the idea of him, which faded even further until all I had was a vague tickle in the back of my mind from time to time. But not anymore. Vincent and I sat around the house that night, fat and happy with knowledge, eating pizza and probably snapping our cards with self-satisfaction. He was out there, and finally we each had someone to talk to about the questions and hopes we were holding on to. I'm not sure we knew in that moment exactly what we were hoping for, but it grew into this: he was real, and we would find him.

Chapter 6—Interrupted (Mark)

Life moved on. It had been many months since Tina and I had last talked about surrogacy. Or adoption for that matter. Work was busy for me at Intel and Tina was rapidly establishing her new career at a Portland-based energy consulting firm. Our time was generally filled by our new jobs. I'm not sure why the most important things in life can so easily be pushed to the back burner. Maybe it's the tyranny of the now. Maybe it's cowardice on our parts. Or perhaps it's some sort of defense mechanism against having to invest the emotional effort needed for the important things. Either way, the transition to living in Oregon easily occupied us, and, per the Children's Aid Society's own estimate, no progress was to be expected on the adoption search front for at least another few years. On the surrogacy front, the challenges seemed as insurmountable as ever, with no navigable path forward. So, we ignored the problem, took good vacations, and did our best to enjoy the quiet life in our grey-blue craftsman home in the suburbs.

Our house backs onto a small, wooded portion of a large local parks and rec facility. Trails through woods were perfect for walking our sweet-tempered hound dog, Evie. Blackberry brambles dominate the edges of the forest paths and anywhere else that they can find sunlight. In the summer they are flush with delicious fruit. Evie generally got far more than we did, but only because she was fearless about plunging through the thorny thickets to retrieve the tasty rewards. Fruit was the perfect prey for Evie, who had trouble with her hips and could no longer lunge at squirrels the way she did when she was younger. Our house was also home to three cats that we had had since we first started dating. Peanut was Tina's grey and white darling. Her fluffiness belied her wilder nature. Aloof and independent, she spent much of her time outside and would curl up at no one's feet but Tina's. Shortly after we arrived in Oregon, Peanut got lost for a four-week adventure across the neighborhood. We eventually spotted her living in a field more than a half-mile from home where she had been sheltering under a small, dilapidated barn, feasting on field mice and the rest of suburban nature's buffet. Millie and Joule were my indoor cats, excessively domesticated, fat, and cuddly. Joule behaved like a small dog—always following me around, sleeping next to me on the bed, and defending the house from strangers and friends alike.

My work required regular travel to California and overseas to Asia, where most Intel-based computers are made. To me, work-travel was a necessary evil of cramped airline seats and budget hotel stays. That said, it helped me connect with the people I worked with in Intel's other offices worldwide, and with our customers. The California trip was the most frequent and happened about once a month. I would fly from the Hillsboro regional airport in Oregon into San Jose International on Intel's dedicated air shuttle service, go straight into the office in Santa Clara, spend one night at the local Plaza Suites, work and network a second day, and then fly home that night— thirty-six hours roundtrip. The Plaza stay included a coupon for three free domestic draft beers at the hotel bar where there was also a free popcorn machine. I usually paid the extra dollar to upgrade my free Budweiser to a more palatable Sierra Nevada. On at least one occasion, the free popcorn and beer made do as dinner.

The morning of that particular California trip began like any other. I was sitting in our home office, finishing up my responses to the previous night's emails and keeping a close eye on the time. I always tried to thread the needle of my departure perfectly, minimizing required waiting around in the small Hillsboro terminal building while not cutting it so close as to risk missing the flight. As usual, my morning email backlog was long. With half my team located many time zones away in Taiwan, Japan, and India, there was always a full workday's worth of messages waiting for me when I first logged on. Other than catching up on those emails, I was ready to go. My minimalist overnight bag was packed and waiting by the front door. Pockets were checked, wallet, keys, and cellphone accounted for, and I was just about to close the lid on my notebook when the home phone rang. It was already 8:28 a.m., this would have to be quick.

"Hello?" I said with a faint touch urgency.

"Hello, is Mark MacDonald there?"

"Yeah, this is him."

"Hi, I'm calling from the Ontario Children's Aid Society."

"Uh, okay." Who? Vague bells went off in the back of my mind, but I couldn't immediately place them.

"I'm calling about your request for a search for your biological mother."

Of course: the adoption search. It had been some three years since I had filed the request paperwork, but as I knew their bureaucracy was geologically slow, it had been far from top of my mind for many, many months. Why were they calling now? There had to be at least a couple of years left before they even began my search. A queasy sensation passed over me as I recalled an article I had read recently in The Globe and Mail, Canada's answer to the New York Times: it reported upcoming changes in Canadian adoption law relating to biological family searches. Hopefully they were calling about some missing detail or form that I needed to provide in order to keep the process moving forward and not to let me know that the request had been cancelled or outright reset somehow by the new laws. I took a long slow breath.

Shaking free the mental cobwebs, I replied, "Yes, that's right. I did request a search, although actually, in addition to finding my biological mother, I was curious about whether or not I might have any part-siblings?"

I paused for another moment, this time to collect myself and to be sure that my message was conveyed—if they were looking, I wanted to be sure they were digging for the right things. There was no immediate response.

"How can I help you?" I ventured.

"Well," said the voice on the line, "we have some good news for you. We have found your biological mother and she would like to meet you too."

Silence. There was nothing I could say to that.

Eventually the voice continued on its own, and for the next three minutes I listened quietly, feeling weak and overwhelmed as something wonderful welled up inside me. Without giving my biological mother's name, the voice recounted fact after fact about her life after my adoption, things not covered in the non-identifying information. It was hard for me to stay focused on each successive piece of information as it was laid before me because I was so busy ingesting each previous morsel. The first and most startling revelation was that my biological mother had married my biological father soon after I was born. They then moved from Ontario to Alberta, where they lived for many years before moving to Kentucky in the US. My biological father had become a pastor, and my biological mother worked in a seminary school. They had three children.

Three children. Full-blooded siblings somewhere out there in the world that I had never met—two brothers and a sister. My life reinvented itself around me in those few moments on the phone. I felt dizzy.

Wait, *pastor*? *Seminary*? These were deeply religious people? It never really occurred to me that my biological roots might be on such a different path than mine.

Parenthetically, my own views on faith are somewhere between atheist and agnostic, and included, at that time, a strong distrust of organized religion, which I viewed as playing a significant role in driving much of the conflict in the history of the world and having the potential to be exploitive at best and oppressive at worst. I had dedicated my own life to science, reason, and pragmatism. Religion wasn't necessarily the enemy but was at best a stranger to me—a stranger that was not implicitly trustworthy.

I stepped back from these details and suddenly realized that in creating the mental image of my biological relatives, I had focused mostly on bracing for "crack whore" or "whereabouts unknown." The potential of a complete family of potentially normal, well-adjusted people with a solid place of their own in the world had seemed like such a long shot that I had not seriously considered it. I was completely unprepared for this. I had no plan, no idea how I would relate to these people or how they might relate to me. I even began to question my own life—was it possible that I was genetically predisposed to do something other than science and engineering? In a few short moments my life's story had suddenly sprouted extra dimensions. There was so much to explore, so much to know, so much to question.

Shit—I'm going to miss my flight.

I had to hurriedly wrap up the phone call, but they left me with the advice to make first contact by letter. That would help temper things a bit and allow us all to ease into this new discovery. I agreed and carefully copied down the particulars for sending such a letter, which would be facilitated by the Children's Aid Society. Before I hung up, I did my best to convey my appreciation for their help. My words were stumbling and honest and did not remotely measure up to the gratitude I felt.

I know I drove myself to the airport that morning, but I have no recollection of the journey itself. From the moment I hung up the phone, I began mentally composing the letter I was to write and the rest of my actions receded into a contented haze along with the rest of the now pedestrian world around me. Putting the words together was more difficult than I imagined. Writing the non-identifying information had been awkward and uncomfortable, but not in an unmanageable way. This was an entirely different animal, tangible and terrifying at a much deeper level. This letter *would* be read. It was not a hypothetical to be filed indefinitely within the annals of the adoption agency, likely never to be seen again. I had some ideas of things I wanted to say, but I couldn't resolve those fragments into a whole. As I struggled, I came to see that my real problem wasn't in the details of the content, but in the conventions of letter writing itself— for example, a salutation and a closing are non-negotiable requirements of a letter. But there are no words to begin a relationship with a stranger who was also your mother, at least none that I could seem to find. This was utterly outside my experience. And beyond the expected anxieties about whether she would like me, or be proud of me, or even respond to the letter, was the unanswerable question of how to sign this letter. Seriously—what closing could I possible use? Love? Sincerely? Cordially Yours? While I wrestled with that question, another unacknowledged and unbidden question lurking in the back of my mind cast a shadow over everything: was this a betrayal of my adoptive parents? I would have to tell them about this at some point. Pandora's Box was open now and things were coming out faster than I could handle them.

Strangely, I also realized in those moments of new connection that I felt even more alone. I was stepping out onto the precipice of something truly new, something that was uniquely for me to experience. It was pulling me out of my life, my known family, and my understanding of the world around me. It was thrusting me, willing or not, into an unknown land. I was traveling with only what I had on me and had no return ticket. At that moment, and for some time afterwards, I felt completely alone.

Chapter 7—First Contact (Rachel)

Easter weekend, 2007. We were living in North Carolina and planning on staying. There's just something about the air and the light down South that I love. It had been eight years since that first revelation from my mom, and my daughters were well ensconced in their childhood. I was a stay-at-home mom, and life was a series of school projects, playing in the backyard, and dinners on the table at 5:00 p.m. We were expecting Mom and Dad for the holiday weekend, but got a rather abrupt call early Saturday morning that they were going to be late, and that when they arrived, we were going to have a family meeting.

Family meetings are nothing new in the Elliott clan. I often call one myself, usually at the dinner table, especially now that I have teenage daughters. It's the only way to make sure everyone knows where everyone else is going, who needs rides, and what The Plan is. When my mom calls them, it's usually because she has a glorious (harebrained) scheme to share. We've had the "we're going to buy a beach house" family meeting, the "we're going to sell the house and move to the lake" family meeting, the "what do you think about sending Kyra to Indonesia to live with your brother Ben for a year?" family meeting . . . It's always best just to smile and nod and wait for the passion to flame itself out. Curtis and I didn't expect anything different to come from this family meeting than any of the others we had attended.

But when Mom and Dad finally arrived, something was different. I don't really know what it was, but maybe it was how they brushed past their granddaughters, or how bags got left in the car for later. It was indefinable, but present. And then:

"He found us."

She sat in my living room, clutching a wrinkled scrap of paper in her hands. Taking a deep breath, her voice cracking, she said, "So, I got a phone call this morning . . ."

Pause.

"It was from an agency that helps adopted children find their birth parents." Here, her eyes welled with tears, and my stomach leapt into my throat. I didn't dare to move or breathe, never mind hope that she was going to say what I hoped she was about to say.

She took a deep breath. "It's why we're late. You remember when I told you about the baby I gave up?"

Was that a real question? Did she honestly think that it had somehow slipped my mind? That I had totally forgotten? That I hadn't spent years searching the faces of men in airports and malls to see if any of them looked like me?

"On the phone this morning, I was told that your brother has been looking for us, that he found us! He found us! Do you want to know his name?" The words were spoken with a lunatic grin. Her eyes were bright with tears and it seemed that her over-wide smile would at any moment give way to sobs. After all those years, to be having this conversation in the normality of my living room, where I watched TV and took naps and folded laundry, seemed mildly insane. My life telescoped down to that room with its long windows, couches and chairs facing each other, and the cat mildly flicking her tail against my hand.

Suddenly, I couldn't get enough air. I couldn't think. I was on the brink of discovering the thing I wanted most in the whole world. I wanted to scream, "Yes! Yes, please, please tell me his name!"

She looked me square in the face, and suddenly we were the only two people in the room. "His name is Mark."

Mark. My world telescoped out again and it felt like I was floating. I had waited so long to hear that name. The name a real person might have, not the name of an illusion. I was brought back to earth by her voice and the realization that I was missing things. She was reading off the facts of his life she had furiously copied onto her scrap of paper while the woman on the phone was speaking. That he had brown hair and blue eyes, he lived in Oregon with his wife, that he was an engineer. All these disconnected facts would become the blocks upon which the reality of my no-longer-secret brother would be built.

And then, more. "Really, he isn't looking for his birth parents. The woman said he's looking for siblings. For you, Rachel, you and your brothers."

I almost laughed out loud! Joy burst through me and all I could think was that I needed to talk to him, see him, know him *right now*. The feeling was so urgent, I was dizzy with it. I immediately asked if I could email him, call him, anything, but I learned I had to wait. He had not yet been notified by the agency that they had, indeed, found his birth parents and three full-blood siblings. There were procedures, a protocol, the worst of which was that whether or not I'd ever be able to contact him was up to him, not me. If he chose to, he could walk away, and I would never get the chance to know Mark. I didn't know what I'd do if that happened.

Late that night, staring up at the ceiling, I marveled at what the day had brought. Sleep was out of the question. So I just lay there, my mind racing. Long after Curtis' breathing settled into the rhythms of sleep, I was running it over and over again in my mind. *Mark. My brother's name is Mark.*

Chapter 8—First Contact (Mark)

I made my California flight despite the extra delay from the Children's Aid Society call. It was an absurd morning emotionally, but I'm always loath to fall short of my commitments. That's just how I was raised, I suppose. I spent the next two days in California and tried my best but was far from productive. Distraction ruled tyrannically over every minute of every hour, impervious to work demands, meetings, or even the free beer at the Plaza Suites. I was composing a letter, first in my mind and then later on paper. Words came out from me slowly as a patchwork of bits and pieces: basic facts, sentiments, and caveats cobbled together, taken apart, rearranged, and then edited over and over and over again. I wrote with extreme self-consciousness. My eagerness was tempered by a hydra of anxieties and insecurities, and in the midst of this maelstrom I found myself confronted by an unexpected question: "Who am I, really?" It was a question I had never really considered explicitly, but writing this letter and trying to be honest about it seemed to demand that of me. My adoptive roots were no longer hypotheticals. Reality was standing on my doorstep and I realized that I would have to come to terms with myself and commit to seeing this through before I went any further. Was I ready to open the door and let reality in? It took all my strength to send the letter, peering through the crack with the chain still in place.

The next few days and weeks brought an explosion of personal correspondence that was unnatural for me, both in scale and in emotional depth. One by one I made contact with the members of my immediate biological family: Marilyn, my biological mother; Steve, the family patriarch and my biological father; Rachel, the oldest of my new siblings, married with two girls of her own; Jordan Vincent, the youngest brother (he had recently decided to go by his middle name, a snap decision to which the rest of the family was still adjusting), an aspiring poet and, I'm told, a living photograph of myself from ten years earlier; and Ben, both the mathematician of the family and probably the most religious—also married and a father of a young boy and another child on the way.

I began writing to them obsessively, with urgency and fear. Nothing else mattered. My life was eclipsed. It was almost embarrassing how quickly and easily the process came to dominate both my work and my home life, subverting my normally steadfast self.

This unraveling and reraveling of my world all began with that first letter from me to Marilyn, cobbled together in a hotel lounge from individual thoughts and sentiments that I had agonized over—every word of it scrutinized and inadequate.

Letter from Mark to biological parents, April 12, 2007

Marilyn and Steve,

Just a short note as a prelude to future conversations. The phone call I received this morning caught me off guard as I was heading to the airport. It has been two or three years since I filed the application for a search to be performed. I imagine that your experience hearing from them was equally surprising—to say the least. I hope that it was not painful or awkward for you to hear from me.

Let me apologize for the typewritten letter—very impersonal. Unfortunately, I have the handwriting skills of a 5th grader (a victim of the digital age), and I also knew this letter would take some editing. At least this message will be legible.

I was pleased to learn that you two are still together. I am really looking forward to meeting you, and getting to know you, and your family. I am particularly interested in someday getting to meet your children. However, I feel I should mention that at this moment I am feeling a little overwhelmed and I am looking to proceed delicately.

[NB: I feel like there is a lawyer somewhere asking me to write this paragraph.] In terms of expectations, I am not looking for anything out of our relationship other than to know who you are and have the opportunity to look at another face that looks like mine. I am also not offering anything other than the opportunity for you to know me and answer any questions you might have. That is not to say that I will seek to avoid any permanent bond or friendship; whatever will be, will be.

One other delicate facet to all this is that I have not informed my parents of my search. I love them and they have always been loving and supportive parents, and open with me about my adoption, but I have decided not to burden them with this knowledge at this time. Although I am sure you are not in contact with them ever, I thought it would be wise to let you know my full situation.

My preference would be to establish contact via email and maybe look forward to setting up a face-to-face meeting sometime in the not-too-distant future. Just in case email is problematic for you for some reason, I am including my full address below. I don't yet know where you are located, but I travel around the country fairly regularly for work, and it should not be too difficult for me to connect with you.

Warm regards and thanks,
Mark

By the time my letter reached its destination, I was back in Oregon, checking my email hourly, and second-guessing every word I had written. Thankfully I only had to wait a handful of forevers before I received a reply.

Letter from Marilyn to Mark, April 16, 2007

Mark—I got your letter today. It was fabulous and terrifying to open it—but in the end it was so sane and kind. Thank you. (I have just deleted the next three things I have tried to write. This is harder than I thought it would be.)

I asked Steve if he would give me the grace of having the initial conversations with you. In a large sense this was my story, borne very much alone.

Like you, I am not grasping for anything from this relationship. I do not have a gaping emotional need I hope to fill. My life has been and is rich at many levels. In some crazy way, though, you have also been part of who I have been and become. How can that be? Just hearing your name was deeply satisfying.

About your folks—I have never been in contact with them nor would I ever. They are yours. Truly they were a gift to me as well as to you. I asked much about them, and felt satisfied in knowing that they were professional, that they had another child, deeply wanted you, and would provide for you in ways I longed to but knew I never could. They have always been my heroes.

I have included a photo of the nuclear family. Do you see any faces that look familiar? At birth you looked startlingly like Ben did at his birth. (Ben is in the middle of both pictures.) But from your description you sound like Steve's family. His dad Vince had red hair . . . and, alas, was quite bald finally.) Rachel is 31, married with two fun girls, living in NC. Jordan is 25 and single—a poet and environmentalist. Ben lives in Calgary with his wife and son, another on the way.

If you can receive it, I would like to write you a letter and just once tell you the story of your birth and launching. Please feel free to ask any questions. I have no idea what you need/want to know. Let me say this—you have great DNA. Our family is strong, healthy, almost no serious medical issues, good brains, and far too much personality. Great genes, that is, except for the nasty male pattern baldness, sorry about that.

We live in Lexington, Kentucky, and also travel a great deal. Most of our married life was lived in Calgary, Alberta. Meeting you will be a great gift to me. But like you, I am happy to go slow.

Just FYI: I did not even entertain the idea of finding you until you were twenty. I was at a retreat when you turned twenty and disclosed my story to a friend for the first time. That began my own journey of remembering and coming to grips with the pain and joy of that season of my life. About four years ago I did some work on the computer to see if there was a way to find you. I even contacted the Toronto Children's Services, who were the adoption agency. I hit a brick wall at every turn. Since then, though, I have quietly waited for the opportunity to find a way through the morass that is the world of adoption. The letter and call from the Adoption Disclosure Unit was a great joy to me. And a shock. We were on our way to visit Rachel, our oldest, and she was greatly excited with us. She would love to write to you but I am making her wait. You will like her. (She said to tell you she is not "LifeTime original movie" eager but very much wants to write to you. I again told her to wait! She is probably looking you up on Google as I speak.)

Mark, connecting with you today is a great joy to me—a real epiphany, my life coming full circle. But I receive it with open hands and no need to control. However this unfolds is good for me. When you feel ready, I'll send you my memories of your birth. Thanks again for writing. It was a great gift. Marilyn

Marilyn Elliott
Community Life
Asbury Theological Seminary
"solvitur ambulando"

Two black and white photos accompanied the message, carefully selected, I'm sure. They showed a contented-looking family on a country porch with broad natural smiles across the board. I searched those faces thoroughly but saw only a family on a sunny porch. I guess I expected more, wanted more, but I felt no immediate connection to the people in these photographs. The parents were completely foreign to me. The man had short curly hair that was starting to recede. The average-built woman held a gentle posture and folksy smile. I suppose I didn't know what I expected to see in their faces exactly. None of them remotely fit the mental image I had of myself. I would soon grow to have a greater appreciation for how inadequately photos of ourselves reflect how we see ourselves or how others see us. Eventually, I would find my own place among these people, or at least beside them, but these photos would remain nothing more to me than a couple of snapshots of a family I hadn't met posing on their porch.

Marilyn, like me, was putting her best foot forward, with a little whitewash, a lot of bravery, and some meaningful details left for later. Comments like "great

DNA" eventually came with a footnote that read: "family history of grand mal epilepsy, and moderate-to-severe depression and anxiety notwithstanding." But her heart was there honestly, every bit of it, like mine was, and was as bare as she could make it. At that point, that is all I wanted or needed. No one starts with their warts.

Letter from Mark to Marilyn, April 17, 2007

Marilyn,

Good Morning :)

Thanks so much for the email and the photos. They are very helpful for me. There are so many interesting parts to respond to that I will never be able to keep a coherent structure here. Again, there has been a lot of editing, so please bear with me. (Also, my sense of humor tends to be sarcastic and pervasive, which does not work particularly well in the written form—so if you see something that doesn't feel right, just assume it is a feeble attempt at humor!)

Let me begin by saying that while I don't want to 'rush' things (not really sure what that means sometimes), I don't see any need from my perspective to impose delays or waiting periods in this process of coming to know a little of each other. I am not an easily overwhelmed person.

Okay, to be fair, I was a little overwhelmed when the Children's Aid called me a couple of weeks ago and told me that they had located you. (But in my defense, I had submitted the request for a search some years prior and had been told that they were no longer conducting new searches because new legislation is being enacted in Ontario.) And I was further overwhelmed when they told me that you and Steve were still together and had other offspring! Bottom line: to me, "not rushing" mostly just means not being a pressure or intrusion on your lives.

It is great to see you doing well and having such a nice family (and such a good looking one—first time I have been able to make that "joke"). My wife (Tina) and I agree that I most closely resemble Jordan; at least these days I do. I have attached a couple of photos of me and Tina, and one with me and my parents taken on our wedding day (June 6, 2000). My hair is still quite thick and not yet receding, so perhaps I am the lucky one? I will hope so!

Rachel is not going to get very far googling "Mark MacDonald"—much too common. My middle name, Angus, gives me my uniqueness, but I don't use it often, so it is not on the web. Also, most of the things that are out there are not particularly interesting to most people. That said, I would love to hear from her and learn more about her and her kids, so a letter would be most welcome!

You wondered what questions I have. That is difficult. Of course, I would like to hear the story of my birth, and the difficult decisions you must have faced. Please send that letter whenever you feel comfortable and have the time to write it. (Recall that in 1973 you filed four or five pages on non-identifying information for me, it will be interesting to see how that compares to the way you see things now, all these years later). Aside from that, I mostly want to know who you and Steve are. And who your children are. Certainly hard to put that in an email-worthy question!

Just a couple of questions to get you started:

Any of your children ever try science/math seriously? Science has always come easily to me. I have always been the one to whom others come for help with their work (both in college and professionally). It always seemed to me to be much more genes than hard work. And my parents are bright but are much more oriented toward the humanities. In many ways, my abilities in this area define me.

Somewhere in the non-identifying information provided to me it said I was born 6 weeks late?! That seems almost impossible. The answer to this question will settle a running dispute between Tina and I as to who is really older :)

Who has the blue eyes? It is hard to tell in the sepia-toned photo!

Where can I get some of Jordan's writing? Is he published? A dear friend of mine is an unpublished poet that teaches music and English at a private high school in California—not an easy way to make a living.

In terms of quid pro quo, I will be happy to answer any questions you have for me (I included a fair bit of stuff in the non-identifying information myself—hopefully you received that?).

A piece of me:

It is 8:30 p.m. on Tuesday. Tina is uncharacteristically absent this evening, on an overnight trip for work to Iowa. I miss her presence, but am content, sitting here in front of my computer with quiet music playing and 17 lbs. of feline affection in my lap (his name is Joule—named after a famous physicist), writing this note to you. Other animals are around.

So many things I could write about. Some questions and stories I will tell next time, and some that should probably wait. But for now, suffice it to say that making this connection has made me feel good. Whole in some sense. You have become real to me. There will be time to fill in the details.

[last two paragraphs rewritten many times]

Let me know what you think in terms of next steps. You mention letter writing, and that is fine (except for my handwriting skills—I have 6 years of elementary school report cards that have "excellent" in every category except for "handwriting," which was always "needs to improve"). I am not a big fan of the phone but would like to meet you and your family someday. I don't make it to Kentucky often (or ever, in fact), and I suspect that you don't spend too much time in the Northwest. How would you feel if I came out to Lexington for a weekend sometime?

Say "hi" to Steve for me :)

Sincerely,

Mark

PS: In the interest of full disclosure, the photos I attached are seven years and thirty pounds out of date.

Letter from Marilyn to Mark, April 18, 2007

Mark—I am looking at the pictures you sent and have to tell you I am crying. And laughing. You ARE Jordan. And you have Ben's eyes. You ask who has the blue eyes—well, all the boys and Steve. Rae and I have dark brown, as do our granddaughters. Ben's boy, Blaise, has blue. When the kids were small it was our family joke that the way we told the boys from the girls in the Elliott house was because the boys had blue eyes. It didn't really speak too highly of any other anatomy, but that's the way it was.

I had your picture up on the screen at work and my assistant walked in and made fun of me for having "Steve's picture" on my screen. You look remarkably like he did a long, long time ago. I have to WARN YOU that I have sent your email and photos to the kids—and you will hear from them. As you describe yourself, so are we. Not much overwhelmed. Not too shy— Jordan and Rachel say that sarcasm is their love language. You get the drift. So please do not be overwhelmed. At least I warned you. This is now out of my control. The game's afoot. I think you are up for it.

I have to tell you a couple other things. Jordan was to get married last year (it didn't happen), but we had ordered kilts from Scotland where Ben was studying (Aberdeen U) and it was going to be a wedding in kilts. We had the Elliott tartan and all the trimmings. I was stunned to see your picture in a kilt.

I will wait a bit to absorb all this and then I will write. I do want to tell you about your beginning. I know Steve will want to talk to you too. I hope you have time to read emails. The intensity of this will not last forever—but this is so great, really. I am glad you feel good about it.

So, the dam is broken and you are going to hear from your irrepressible siblings. Mark, the thing is this. You are not a stranger to us.

This is so . . . something.

Warmly,

Marilyn

P.S: Steve says hi. (I attached his picture because it is your future—like looking into a mirror. And a picture of our girls. Personality plus.)

As Marilyn promised, I did hear from my siblings promptly. Over the next forty-eight hours I wrote more and felt more than I had in any two-day period of my life. It was a little overwhelming, but not overpoweringly so. Messages kept smiling at me from my inbox and I kept smiling back.

Chapter 9—Reaching Out (Rachel)

It took over a week for the ability to contact Mark to finally filter down to me. It was agonizing. But then it happened when I least expected it.

I remember it vividly: I was singing in church the following Sunday, so I was at rehearsal, standing on the platform in a windowless, storefront church sanctuary, with my team—all friends, all who knew that I was waiting. I loved singing on the worship team and was a happy camper, goofing with Josh while Kyra & Meg climbed over chairs and slithered through the aisles (as bored kids are wont to do). Curtis went back to the sound board to check on something or maybe turn the magical dials and happened to see a notification pop on his phone. It was a text from my mom, to both of us, that we should check our email.

Curtis pulled the email up on the laptop that ran the sound board, and there was a grin on his face when he looked up and said, "Do you want to see this?"

I immediately went to hop off the stage, but he told me to turn around. There, on the screen behind me, larger than life, he had projected Mark's image.

I froze. And then I burst into tears. Kyra and Meg stood still. I can't begin to describe how it felt to look at him for the first time in my life. He had the face of my father and baby brother, almost exactly. I don't know why I didn't expect that, but I didn't. It knocked the wind right out of me. I could have picked him out of the airport or the mall or the crowd at the state fair. It was a face I already knew and loved—how could I not love him, too? There was a mystical thing that happened when my daughters were born; my heart expanded, almost physically, with love. That is exactly what happened when I looked at his picture. I still didn't know much more than his name, but I loved him. Immensely.

Staying at rehearsal was not an option. Curtis waved me out the door, saying he'd keep The Girls so that I could have time to myself to use the email address at the bottom of the photograph. My heart raced during the fifteen-minute drive home down Durham's winding back roads, and I had that prickly, crazy-nervous sweat all over. Once in the garage door, my purse was summarily dumped on the floor as I immediately grabbed my laptop, pausing only to pour a generous glass of *vinho verde*. With a deep breath, I bravely opened my email and started a new message. I copied and pasted his email address, and . . . *gulp*.

Mindlessly swirling my glass, I sat in front of the blinking cursor. How do you write your first letter to the brother you've never known but love beyond explanation? How do you fit thirty years of life onto paper so *you* can be known? What are the things you need to say in order to give a clear picture of who you are? And how on earth do you do all that without scaring him away? I typed and deleted, typed and deleted, drank and typed and deleted. Finally, several glasses of wine and three full email drafts later, I finally came to what I hoped was just right—not too emotional, not too overwhelming. Pushing send was the boldest thing I had ever done.

Letter from Rachel to Mark, April 18, 2007

Dear Mark,

I have to start off by saying that this is so exciting! (I had many other, more weighty & impressive introductory sentences, but I decided to go with "simple and honest.") This is, in fact, the third email I've composed . . . (eep!). I grew up without knowing that you were out there in the world and discovering that you are is a tremendous gift to me. Maybe that seems odd to you, but there it is. Because I love my family. They are crazy, wonderful, loud, funny, creative, thoughtful, stubborn, intelligent, loyal, and fierce. And then I saw a picture of you today and burst into tears—I recognized in yours the faces of men I already love so much. I was seized with a great affection—you are my brother. Having you in my life only adds to its richness! I have such a smile on my face, you probably wouldn't believe it! Suddenly, I find myself a girl with 3 brothers! An older brother! How crazy cool is that?

I was moved by the statement in your letter to my parents that you aren't offering anything but the chance to know you— from where I stand, that is a huge offering! The opportunity to get to know you, to become friends, to come to the day when we are comfortable being brother and sister—this is a remarkable gift! Neither of us knows how this works, I guess, but my bottom line is that there is as much space in my life for you as you would like to have! (sorry for the overuse of exclamation points—I can't seem to help myself tonight)

I laughed at your self-description. The expression I heard (3[d] hand, so forgive me if it's not exact) was "strong personality." You could say that about all of us, really. None of us has ever been accused of being a wallflower! Also, where you mentioned sarcasm—Jordan and I like to say that sarcasm is our "love language." (My husband, Curtis, says that we say things to each other in our family that he would never in a million years say to his worst enemy! But they are all said with heaps of affection and humor!) I want to tell you about myself, but I'm not sure how to do it without either sounding like a personal ad or coming across like someone padding a resume. It's easiest to start by saying that I would describe myself much the way you described yourself. Loud, funny & sarcastic—and I will add that I love life & living things, music & art, people, good books, and my hammock.

We are all pretty smart, but I was never any good at math. The biological sciences are something both Jordan and I delved into—he as a vet student and me as a nursing student (although neither of us graduated with those degrees). I love to speak and teach, and if I have an opinion I will happily give it, solicited or not. I love beauty in all its forms—nature, art, writing (Jordan is an amazing poet, btw, with his first book coming to a Barnes & Noble near you on May 28! Death by Love at First Sight, *under the name J. Vincent Elliott), music, animals, et al—and would rather be outside than inside 9 times out of 10 (the exception being the cold. I hate the cold!).*

I love to throw a great party, where people come and laugh and drink and eat and stay late. I am useless without coffee in the morning. I love my daughters, Kyra—the kind and thoughtful one, and Meg—the charismatic and emotional one. I love our cats, Satchmo (after Louis Armstrong) and Holidae (after Billie Holiday). I maintain two goldfish (Chubby Pants & Col. Rev. Dr. Capt. Chips), because I got a random fishbowl (Curtis just read that, and swears it was "thoughtful") for Christmas two years ago and I think all life deserves to be nurtured. I love to sing at events with my husband—weddings, New Year's things, hotel lobbies, etc. I love to get dressed up and go out for martinis with friends, to stay on the couch in my pjs and watch House *or* The Office, *and I especially love summer days laying in my hammock listening to the birds and The Girls* and the lawn mower. I am a voracious reader, even if none of my favorite books pass Jordan's inspection (he is a lover of Literature). On August 6, I will have been married for 13 years—hooray for us! I still love my husband, and hope that Meg (who really is a mini "me," to both her great benefit & detriment) finds a man just like him.

I know that negotiating this new and unfolding relationship will be a process, not an event. It's just that it's a process I am very much looking forward to! I will try hard to not overwhelm, but I too am bestowed with a strong personality and my joy is difficult to keep in check! I eagerly anticipate what the future has to hold, and hope that we become great friends. (Also, I need you to know that I am perfectly content to have our relationship stand independent of any relationship you develop with my parents, if that's what you prefer.)

There are so many conversations I want to have with you—I am tempted to pour them all out right now—but I will listen to my mother (*gasp!*) and wait. I look forward to hearing from you, to meeting you (do you ever travel to the Research Triangle in NC? Or if you come to KY to meet Steve and Marilyn, can I come?), and to all the future conversations we will have . . .

With great affection, your sister,
Rachel

(I was going to put "love" but it seemed too forward—ha!)

Chapter 10—The Game's Afoot (Mark)

Everything about first contact with the new siblings was unnaturally fun for me, despite the many deep questions it raised. In my experience as an adopted person, I always felt a sense of purity with regard to the "nature" side of my own nature-versus-nurture dichotomy. The nature part came in only one flavor—the one I have always known as simply me. Math and science come easily to me. I'm a fast runner. I'm shy with girls, enjoy sarcastic humor, and don't have the patience for arts or crafts. I believed these aspects of myself to be fundamentally tied to my DNA—clear and immutable. Without knowing any biological relations, I had never had the chance to see how the same genetic traits could manifest differently in someone else who shared the same core instruction set. Discovering the existence of similar yet different biological relatives brought those fundamental certainties into question for me. While building new bonds with them made me feel more connected and more balanced as a person, at the same time it threatened to upend the naïve emotional foundations upon which I had built myself.

The same evening that I received first contact from Rachel, I also heard from Ben, the middle son. His letter was more structured, more distant, but also openly welcoming and rife with evidence of his sharp wit. Later I learned that Ben was the only one of the children that had never previously been told of my existence. I cannot imagine the emotional labyrinth he must have had to negotiate that week. I obliged his playful demand to respond to his note first, but it was my exchanges with Rachel that formed the deepest and most meaningful connections.

Letter from Mark to Rachel, April 18, 2007

Rachel,

Wow.

Before I get started here, let me begin by apologizing for responding to Ben's email first, but he promised me a case of scotch and threatened to let the air out of my tires—forgive my weakness.

I loved your note. And I am having the same problem with editing (both my emotions and my sarcasm). I am not really sure how to deal with the concept of "sister," but I will do my best. :) Should I call you Little Sis? Just kidding. Seriously, the sister thing throws me for a loop and so does the age difference (I am the youngest in my family—one older brother).

I want to know you and your family. I am so glad you exist, and so glad you are happy. Your girls are beautiful. Tina and I don't have any kids yet (there is a story there; one that is related to why I started searching for your parents in the first place, but I will wait on the telling of it. Nothing sinister, just not right for email).

Cool that you are into classic jazz (inference based on cats). My musical tastes are a little all over the place, but Louis Armstrong's "Wonderful World" was our wedding song.

I like reading too, but am slow as molasses. I try to alternate between "literature" and "fun" reading, but I really prefer the fun. If you are looking for something lighthearted, but well written, I recently discovered Christopher Moore and have enjoyed his work thoroughly (note: two things I have not even mentioned so far in my emails-to-the-Elliotts are politics and religion, probably best to know each other a little better first? But I feel obliged to note that one of Moore's books, Lamb, *probably counts as blasphemy—so maybe read one of his others first?).*

We do have pets. Three cats and one dog. The cats are not slim. Joule (cat) peaked at about 18 lbs. We call him "Fatty" (affectionately). Or "Blubber Puss." Or, when he is meowing for food at 6:00 a.m. (as he is doing behind me as I write this), "Mr. Annoying Pants." Not sure where the 'pants' comes from—interesting to hear about your goldfish's moniker! Joule and his sister, Millie, both look like bags of water flapping around when they run. It is really rather sad—but they have been on nothing but diet food since six months of age (nine years ago).

Tina and I are both big on being outdoors. Hiking, canoeing, and exploring. Mostly low key, communing with nature kind of stuff. And who doesn't like The Office*? When I first saw the scene where Jim and Pam put Dwight's desk set in the vending machine, I nearly fell off the sofa. And I adore my pajama pants. I am currently wearing flannel polar bears.*

I need to sign off soon. Tina will be arriving home from a business trip any minute. I promise to write again soon with more details. Do you have any questions for me? We can talk about anything you like. Bring it on. :)

In answer to the questions you did mention: yes, I am hoping to visit Marilyn and Steve in KY if they are comfortable with that. And yes, I would love to meet you face-to-face as well. Either there or in NC or anywhere that works out. I don't get to go to Triangle Park for work (I used to have a friend that worked there, but that was some time ago), but I won't need a better excuse.

79

Your letter has touched me deeply. You and your family are more than I hoped for when I started this journey. I can't wait to see where it will take us next.

Your big brother,
Mark

Chapter 11—Meeting A Family from The Inside (Mark)

My biological family and I were tiptoeing out onto the frozen pond together, not sure if the ice would hold. We were brave and hopeful. Optimistic. Braggarts. And still not without the odd sin of omission—but those were only minor transgressions, little white lies to smooth the way until we could trust one another with our baggage as well as our hearts. The correspondence we had in those first weeks made me glad at my core. Checking my email each day was like a child's Christmas morning—glorious anticipation and anxious tension at once. It was the best of times.

Letter from Mark to Marilyn, April 19, 2007

Marilyn and Steve,

Well, I have heard from all your kids. You have clearly done a wonderful job of raising them. They are so friendly, so warm and inviting. So willing to welcome me into their inner circle. I cannot remember the last time I have felt this moved. I am probably most like Ben, but Rachel and Jordan (Vincent? J. Vo?) reflect other sides of me (the less nourished sides?), and it has already been an incredibly rewarding experience to meet them. It must have been difficult for them to learn about me and my finding you, but they do not show it. I am very much looking forward to building friendships with each of them.

The kilt is one of my favorite outfits. I have worn it to at least a couple of weddings (in addition to my own) and even a couple of office Christmas parties. In the non-identifying information I got, there was a description of a (fabled?) relation to Bonny Prince Charlie—any truth to that?

I agree that this is a crazy sort of burst of joy; and certainly, it will not last forever. My hope is that after we know each other's faults as well as our strengths, our failures as well as our triumphs, and our fears as well as our hopes, that there will be a lasting bond that will be just as satisfying as this flurry of excitement.

Know that I have never had any regrets about my life. I have been afforded every advantage and built more opportunities for myself than I will ever be able to make use of. I have almost always been happy, hopeful, and content. That said, adding you and your family to my life has made me happier still. I am so glad I found you—regardless of what comes of this.

Mild warning: know also that if and when you meet me in person, do not expect me to be so forthcoming with my feelings. One of my shortcomings is that I am not good about talking about things like that. (That is one of the reasons I chose email for first contact, and why I prefer face-to-face over phone calls :)). I just want to level-set expectations. I certainly feel things, and in the right mood, I can write them down, but I have trouble verbalizing my feelings. Selective shyness, I suppose.

I am looking forward to your next note, and to the story of my birth, and to word from Steve, and to meeting you both someday. But take your time. This is certainly a lot for me to absorb also! At some point I will need to fill you in on my decision to search for you—there is a bit of a complicated story for that one. One that I look forward to sharing, but I would like to hear your story first, if that is ok.

[no idea what closing is appropriate here—that selective shyness is setting in]

Mark

Chapter 12—Unintended Pain (Mark)

I knew in my heart that the search wasn't about my parents, but it certainly related to them. They have always been good parents and have afforded me every opportunity in life and no end of support—I owed them the truth. At some point in this process, I needed to tell my parents about the adoption search. I was hesitant, because surely an adopted person seeking out their biological roots is inherently a betrayal of their adoptive family at some level, whether or not that was how it was intended. Having to let them know was tragic, but unavoidable. The best I could do was be honest, hope for understanding, and hope that the knife did not cut too deeply. So, on a Sunday afternoon in May I told them what I had searched for and what I had found. I told them gingerly, during one of our scheduled weekly calls, and they gave every appearance of taking it well. I'm not sure how I expected them to take it.

The conversation itself was not easy for me, nor for them, I expect. There were many pauses, but also many accepting acknowledgements and supportive murmurs. My parents are not effusively emotional people. They are polite. Their love languages are steadfastness and tradition. They are *not* Elliotts. My home growing up was one of a less tangible sense of love than some, but I think not less in quality or quantity. Spontaneous hugs were seldom seen. But love was clearly seen in the rigor of our family. Saying "goodnight" was saying "I love you" at the end of each and every day—not saying "goodnight" would be an unthinkable offense.

These days I don't talk to my parents that often, save for the weekly calls that have been going on as long as I can remember, and not all of those calls forge true connections. Many times, I would lack the emotional energy to really try. But this week the call was not the usual and so I mustered all I could. I knew I had to connect into them in order for me to tell my story honestly and gently. I felt sad to have to bring it up with them at all, and I did not know how I might console them if they came out hurt. But as I say, they seemed to take it well.

In the spirit of openness, and with hopes of ameliorating any injury I might have inflicted, I tried to be more engaged on all our calls after that, and more open about the daily comings and goings of my Oregon world—which were undoubtedly opaque to them in Toronto. I wanted them to know that I was merely exploring myself on this journey and not turning away from our family unit. But the mechanisms to have that conversation did not really exist within our familial lexicon. So, I did what I could within the bounds of what I knew. And within the bounds of what my thirty-five-year-old, overly pragmatic, engineering-scientist heart could handle.

My life in the days and weeks that followed was undermined by guilt and awkwardness. I searched for other ways to bridge the divide that I felt I had created. Humor being somewhat of a love language for me, I decided to try sharing with my parents in that spirit— something that I had rarely done in the past, perhaps because of their formality, or perhaps because of my awkward shyness around formal people. They prefer classical music, poetry, literature, and the finer arts. They do not generally share my comedic taste. But I came across a particular video spoof that the website *JibJab* had created. To me it was hilarious in a way they would also appreciate and I decided to use it as an olive branch.

The spoof was made about the time that Prime Minister Tony Blair was being replaced in the UK, and they had mixed clips of both Blair and then–US President George W. Bush, making it appear that they were singing each other a love song duet of a farewell—satirically poking fun at their relationship as key allies in Iraq among other things. Being funny, political, and British (my mother hails from the UK), I thought my parents might find a smile in it and that it might ease some of the tension I felt from the family. So, breaking with tradition, I forwarded a copy of the video to them via email. Per my usual habits, I did not include any explanatory cover note. They both follow politics closely, so I assumed they would immediately get the context and simply appreciate the satire. I should have thought it through better.

I received a response from them a few days later letting me know that they had watched the video together several times. They told me that they had "turned off the silly images and closed their eyes and just listened to the song." The blood drained from my face and my stomach contorted. The song was a schmaltzy piece of garbage—a *farewell love song.* They thought I was saying goodbye to them. I did not know what was worse, that I had made them think I was saying goodbye, or that they could believe that I would say goodbye, or that I could possibly ever do it in such a ridiculous manner. Either way a truth was revealed. This was no scratch. This was a chasm ripped through the center of our well-tended, peaceful family garden. The damage wrought might take a lifetime to repair.

So it was that in those first weeks and months when I came to know Marilyn, Rachel, Vincent, Ben, and Steve, and my heart grew in a way that I never thought possible, another older, equally precious part of my heart was broken.

Chapter 13—Making New Family (Rachel)

There's this thing that whales do—echolocation. It's the way they "sing" underwater by using sonic pulses to tell where the other whales in the pod are, and it's how they keep track of one another. Email became my sonic pulse; I couldn't let a day go by without sending my "song" out into the cyber-ocean. I needed to know that Mark was still there, still real. We were separated by thousands of miles—North Carolina to Oregon is almost as far as you can get in this country! —and hadn't yet met, so I carried a small, little fear that once again he would fade before my eyes.

In one of our early emails, he sent me an invitation to use the Google Talk IM tool. I immediately signed myself up, wanting every possible link I could get. Once I had gone through all the "confirm password" stuff, the IM box opened on my desktop, and there, under contacts, was "Mark MacDonald." Terrifyingly, his button was green. He was online right at that moment. It was entirely possible that he was looking at my green button. I was paralyzed. The prospect of real time conversation left me flushed and shaken as I continued to stare at my laptop's screen. I couldn't get over the fact that he was right there, at the other end of that connection. As I sat, trying to will myself into the courage to type, a small bell sounded and a dialogue box opened.

It read, "Boo."

Just like that, the spell was broken. I laughed out loud and thought that a more perfect opening line could not exist.

Chapter 14—A Package in The Mail (Mark)

I got home from work one day that spring and found a small brown envelope from Marilyn in our mailbox. She had sent me an email warning a couple of days prior that "a package" was coming. I nested the envelope among the pile of other mail that I collected from the box and brought it into the house along with my work bag and a few groceries that I had stopped to pick up on the way home. It had been a typical day at the office—meetings, phone calls, analysis—but now I was home and it was time to walk the dog, unwind a little, and start to think about what to do for dinner.

I unloaded the groceries and the mail in a pile on the kitchen island counter. I picked up the brown envelope and placed it deliberately aside, face up and aligned with its edges true to the black granite tiles of the countertop before turning back to the detritus of other mail and the perishable food items that ought to be sequestered away into the fridge for safe keeping. I paused for a moment and heard only my breath. Then I slowly began to unpack the groceries. Working mechanically, carefully, each individual item was placed into its correct location in the pantry or fridge until all were stowed. It was a surreal dance that moved with the languid purposefulness of a celestial orbit. To this day I don't know whether it was avoidance or the thrill of building anticipation that was guiding my behavior. As I worked, I would steal glances at the brown envelope with my name on it.

With the groceries put away, I turned next to the pile of other mail, sorting through one by one until all were placed in the recycling.

Then I stood alone in our quiet home. Tina was still on her way home from work. It felt like there was some sort of slim journal or notepad tucked inside the envelope. I opened the seal trepidatiously. I could now sense Marilyn's emotional baggage glowing through the plain brown wrapper. This was not what I had been looking for. I had no real interest in resolving her issues—I just wanted to know my roots, my siblings.

I pulled the notebook out of the envelope, and a yellowed piece of folded paper came free and wafted to the floor like a kite without a string. I picked up the paper and unfolded it—a letter from the Children's Aid Society of Metropolitan Toronto. It read:

Letter to Marilyn, undated

Miss Marilyn Christie

346 East 37ᵗʰ Street

Hamilton, Ontario

Dear Marilyn:

I am glad to be able to tell you that Stephen's adoption was finalized last year, and though the social worker who placed him has left the Agency, I have her notes which she left on the record. She described him as a bright child. He was a bit fretful the first month after he was placed with his adoptive parents, but when he settled down, he became a happy, responsive child. He is big, solid, and "all boy." He was doing well when the adoption was made final.

I think I told you that his new father is a professional person and both he and his wife are the kind of people who can give stimulation to a child. They were experienced parents when Stephen was placed with them. Apparently, all the relatives and friends were very much attracted to Stephen, too.

I hope what I can tell you will help, Marilyn, as you think about Stephen. Give my regards to Stephen Sr. You have my very best wishes for happiness in your coming marriage.

Yours sincerely,

(Miss) E. Lemon

I put the letter down on top of the now empty envelope and turned to the notebook, a plain, small scratchpad of lined paper tied up in a simple straw ribbon, about twenty-five pages total, with the first half dozen already ripped out. I untied the ribbon and lifted the mahogany brown cover page. Inside, along with several pages of handwriting, I discovered a typed cover letter on a plain 8 ½ x 11 piece of paper:

Letter from Marilyn to Mark, April 18, 2007

Mark,

This little package is necessary for me to do this connection rightly. I have no idea if you need or want to hear this story like I can tell it. After we connected, but before I saw your picture, I went alone to a retreat center, my personal refuge, and sat for hours by a pond and thought and cried and wrote. What I wrote is in the enclosed notepad. It is a first draft—very messy. But I choose not to refine it. The story is ragged. So be it.

I have huge reservations sending this to you. I don't want to impose on you what you might not want to receive. But this has been in my heart to say since January 1973.

To help you I have found a picture of me taken when I was sixteen, shortly after your birth. This is the girl who held you when you were born. This is the girl's heart that you heard as a lubdub *when your ears first comforted to sound. Somehow, I thought it might help if you had a face to connect to the story. Maybe make it real.*

The first half of the story, as I reread it, is really written by this girl. To say it is a story of a life and death struggle is not to over-dramatize. But also, it is a story of beauty out of context. Your life, and mine, are and were beautiful. Our story, Steve's and mine, is not a story of a sordid life. There were no drugs or alcohol, no abuse or mental illness, no promiscuity. He was a disciplined athlete and I was a vital girl. Your birth was not celebrated in a beautiful way, except in this girl's heart, until at last you were with your adoptive family (and may I say, I loved that I have seen their faces in your wedding picture) and your chances really began.

The second half of what I have written, as I reread it, (this was not consciously planned) is from me, now. It is my heart for you as a man today. Maybe that is what I dread sending you. I want you to know that what I have written is very deep, very true to who I am and how I process life, but in no way presumes that you need me in any way, or even need to hear what I have to say. I just once have to say it.

(I have no idea how this will line up with the previous info you have. You were not six weeks overdue—horrors. You were two weeks overdue, like all my other children.)

So this is sort of my caveat . . . to say that for me *this is an important piece of knowing and being known. But also to affirm that this is not where I want to stay, not what I want to dwell on. I guess, frankly, I fear your rejection.*

So . . . because so much is at stake, here it is.

Handwritten at the bottom of that last page was "This is very good—Marilyn."

I moved on to the handwritten pages of the notebook itself:

Journal entry, Marilyn, Loretto Motherhouse, Nerinx, KY, April 16, 2007

I first laid eyes on Steve Elliott in the hallway of Barton High in Hamilton, 1971. I was almost 15, in Grade 10. He was a senior, tall and lean, with a big head of curly hair and an athletic look. We made eye contact across the foyer but did not speak. A day later he called me at home and asked me out. I said yes without knowing his name. I knew who he was, of course.

We had great chemistry and tons of fun. We laughed, played, ran, joked, and created adventures in everything. (Steve had just recovered from extensive knee surgery when we met, and still holds several records in cross country and sprints. I never saw him run.) He is 5 years older.

Within that first year I became pregnant. It was the early '70s and being "unwed" and pregnant was a great shame. (Do they even use the term "unwed" anymore?)

I went to a doctor who talked to me about abortion. It was getting easier to have abortions by then. I decided to talk to my parents and that turned out badly. Steve was great and stayed close. But in the end, I had to leave and go somewhere else if I was to have this baby. I was very much alone.

I went to Toronto and lived here and there until I stumbled into a "home for girls." I found a little office job and lived the last trimester at the "home." You don't need to hear all that experience so I will move to your birth. ~

(By the way—did you know that the word "delivered" in relation to birth refers to the mother? It is the mother who is delivered from the child—or she would die—and the child is born.)

The nurses at the hospital generally treated me with disdain. They knew I had chosen to give this baby up. And again, the shame of being "unwed." The doctor who delivered you (—me!—) was young and kind to me. I was alone and his kindness was precious to me. (He helped me survive.)

When you were born—a boy!—they would not let me see you. The nurses whisked you away and told me it was better if I never saw you. I was compliant and overwhelmed.

They put me into a room with three nursing moms. It was morning. By lunch I could not bear it and I asked if I could give you your next feeding. The answer was yes. I realize now that they couldn't deny me anything related to you but they didn't offer anything either.

You were brought in a while later, and I held you and fed you. I began to cry, holding you close. I sobbed and sobbed, so loud and so long that the nurse came in and snatched you out of my arms and told me I was disturbing the ward. She was the worst of the nurses.

She came back and led me, still crying, to a small (8' x 8' or so) room with a two-person seat and another chair, one wall picture of a ship sailing some sea, and a window. It was some kind of consultation room. They left me there alone. I curled up on the couch and cried 'til I slept. When I woke the room was pitch black. I looked up and saw stars out the window. After a bit I got myself up and found my room and slept, exhausted.

In the morning I got dressed, called Steve in Hamilton and asked him to find a way to get me, and I checked myself out of the hospital. Previously I had arranged with the Toronto Children's Services to find a family. They told me about your chosen family. I asked a lot of questions and was finally satisfied that this was a good place.

When Steve came, I asked to see you again. The nurse brought you to me, clearly against her better judgement. (Does judgement have an "e"?) Steve and I unwrapped you and marveled at your soft perfection. You grabbed our fingers—a sign of intelligence I hear—and didn't cry. I kissed you and smelled you, trying to breathe you right into my soul. Then I let you go. (I cry now to write this.) I never expected to see you again. It had to be final.

You know, Mark, that babies are adopted for many reasons and failings. But when I gave you, I knew you were a prince. You were my Moses. It was not safe for me to keep you. But I knew you were <u>strong</u> and <u>whole</u>. You would make it—fragile now but I willed <u>fierce</u> strength into you. I was sure that you were unique and amazing already—no flaws.

There was a period of time when a birth mother could change her mind and reclaim the child. I knew that. It made everyone nervous. I also knew I would never do that. I had to be fierce, too, to survive. I wrote 2 letters to the adoption agency during the time before the adoption was final. I had to hear if you were ok. I received one reply which I have kept these 34 years—I think to prove to myself that you were real and not a dream. I'm sending it to you. I don't need it anymore.

In the years that followed, when our other children were growing, and they would make us howl with laughter or burst with pride over an insight or accomplishment, I would often *think of you and smile inside my soul. I would imagine you <u>amazing</u> your parents or making them laugh. I have always pictured them being so proud of you and thinking themselves remarkably blessed to have been given a son like you. Then I would breathe a small prayer for you—that you would be protected and made strong and noble—fierce.*

Mark, you were conceived on the cusp of a great, joyous (albeit young) love. We have always been together, Steve and I. I can imagine no other life. You are right at the heart of that love, although you were torn from it. (I died to you so you could live.)

Having said all this—all of it, candidly, <u>true</u> and vulnerably spoken (because this you deserve)—let me add that I am keenly aware that I do not possess you or any right to you, in any way. I would never violate the sacredness of your personal journey, or even desire that you would change in <u>any</u> way to accommodate me (us). Rather, this is a real invitation to you—to . . . (I am thinking long how to say this) . . . It is an invitation to come and see and know (to the level you want) your people. And to let us see and know you. I truly believe this can be a healthy and life-giving quest for us all. You are <u>not</u> a stranger to us.

In writing this I mostly want you to see and feel that you have <u>always</u> been cherished, even though you have no memory or participation in that love. It has been (I so hope) a blessing over your life, intangible but real.

To completely release you into another woman's hands and walk away, anonymous, into the crowd, was the loneliest moment of my life. The only thing I can imagine could be lonelier is death.

But it is all given back! All is made good. Our lives are ragged—yes, but blessed also. This letter (which I never <u>dared</u> dream I would write) is proof of it.

This is a first draft—unedited, no spell check—I wanted to write with my own hand. I am sitting by a pond at a retreat house and the sun is setting behind me. My thoughts have been unguarded. (I reread some of this and I sound 15 again—not 50).

We make choices and those choices turn around and make us.

Judge me tenderly,

Marilyn

your birth mother

I was sobbing quietly well before I finished reading, and now my body wracked as I doubled over, staggered by the words I had read. Tears coursing mercilessly from my eyes. I have not cried like that before or since in my life. Even as I stood there shaking, I was not entirely sure why I was crying. It was a half hour before I could compose myself. Clearly, I had more emotional issues connected to being adopted than my mind had let on. I braced myself for the journey yet to come and set about making dinner for Tina and me, trying to find some comfort in the ordinary.

Later that night, I struggled. I struggled emotionally, not able to share the contents of the envelope with Tina—my closest partner in this life. And I struggled to find a response that I could send to Marilyn, though I knew she would be waiting on one desperately.

Letter from Mark to Marilyn, April 21, 2007

Marilyn,

I have the package.

I have no words for how much that meant to me. I am surrounded by Kleenex and will need some time to compose myself before responding properly.

For now, know that there is no judgment [spell check]. There never was. The child in me is grateful for the difficult choices you made. The man is proud of the strength and courage you showed in a situation I can barely imagine.

I am crying again and need to stop writing. You will hear from me soon.

love,

Mark

Chapter 15—Calgary (Mark)

As it happened, Marilyn and Steve were traveling to Calgary for work the following week, and being a short flight from Portland, it seemed like a good opportunity for our first face-to-face encounter. We decided that I would meet them there for an overnight visit at neutral locale—a hotel in the nearby resort town of Banff.

In the days leading up to the visit, the shock of reality would occasionally break through my hazy joy of anticipation, and there was no lack of panicking. Feelings came to me in waves of anticipation, anxiety, and peace. I had trouble focusing on anything. Marilyn's week was little different.

Letter from Marilyn to Mark, April 23, 2007 (morning)

Mark—do you have time to read another email? This is for me . . . let me just do some random consciousness.

We have created a sort of intensely personal yet still abstract relationship. I have told you things I haven't even told Steve. And now I want to flee. Here's the thing. I am pretty much fearless in all I do. If I am afraid, I just confront it and move on. But now I am something like afraid and my "strategies" are not helping me. I think, as I try to be honest with myself, that I fear you will find me irrelevant or boring or . . . what? (My fear is not in how I will find you to be, but in how you will find me.)

For the first time in my life, I don't know who I am in this circumstance. I am not a mother; I don't want to be a mother. I am not a friend. It feels like more than a friend. I am not an aunt or professor or mentor or guide. I know how to be all those things. I don't know how to be this.

So, I don't feel stable. Do you want to meet an unstable woman? LOL The last thing I want to do is to negatively impact your life. You will probably never ever be able to comprehend how much pure joy I feel in the strength and wellness I perceive in your life.

I guess what I am saying, because I am in such foreign land, is that I want you to see me as bulletproof and worth knowing, and I know I am not bulletproof and wonder, now, if I am even interesting. ARGH!!!!!! It is like instead of living inside my life I am living outside analyzing it from the edges. A Hungarian philosopher and writer said that "in his bedroom, no man's fame bears inspection." That quote has come to me this weekend.

I guess, Mark, that this means so much to me, it feels like so much is at stake, that I am unsure how to be in it. Can you relate to this in any way? You have been nothing but gracious to me (us). You have been open and kindly received more than I imagined you could. (I really think I did not breath for two days when I sent you my letter. That you received it tenderly was such a gift to me.)

This is another risk, to write you my thoughts today. Time together will help me. I know at a deep level that what is to be will unfold . . . I am pretty good at not controlling and receiving what is.

Don't interpret this as me not wanting to be with you in Calgary. Nothing could be further from the truth. I am just slightly terrified (oxymoron ;-)).

I am writing this because I am trying to trust my instincts and I am not getting any work done anyway. Marilyn

Letter from Mark to Marilyn, April 23, 2007 (midday)

Marilyn,

Telling the truth is never a bad thing. We have all been putting our best foot forward in this, and trying to stifle our trepidation; I think that is the right thing to do in many ways too.

Of course, honesty begets honesty. And to try and allay your fears (a perhaps futile effort?), I will say that you are not the only one who feels insecure about this meeting. This is not an easy thing for me to say, but given what you have done for me in the last week, I know that I owe you at least this much. More than anything, I want you to find me to be a good man, a happy man, and a successful man (it might be arrogance, but I believe each of these things to be true about myself); I want you to be proud of the person I have become. But that is a tall order to fill . . . And I fear that my lack of religion will make me unworthy to you. I also fear any number of known and unknown differences or failings I have.

I have no concerns over what I will find you to be. I know you will be different from me and yet the same. I will take you as you are and be glad of it. The only reason I could write the previous paragraph is that I believe (hope?) that you are like me and will take me as I am as well.

I am not looking for a substitute family—I have a family already that has taken great care of me with love and support for 34 years. But I am thrilled at this chance to add a supplemental family, one that connects me to the rest of the world in a way I have never been able to fully understand.

Words like "irrelevant" and "boring" have no place on your page. Can you conceive of anything I could do or say (or have done or said) that would make me seem irrelevant or boring to you?

Yes, it is scary. And yes, it is exciting and joyful and thrilling and everything else. But you can release your fears because we are tied to this fate together. You and I. [pausing to think about the "you" and the "I" in that sentence is starting to bring a tear to my eye again—apologies because I know it will likely do the same to you.] I feel the same fears in my own ways, so we should at least find comfort that we are in the same boat.

I am anxiously looking forward to five minutes of trauma followed by twenty-four hours of pure enjoyment and discovery in Calgary. As well as a lifetime of connected friendship (I have no idea what words to use for that concept either!) afterwards.

Now take a deep breath and get back to work! I know that is what I need to do. :)

Mark

Letter from Marilyn to Mark, April 23, 2007 (afternoon)

Right. Get back to work. This is the nicest email I have ever received and now I am supposed to get back to work. I have to hire three people this afternoon and teach a class tonight that I have not prepared for—but I can't be present to any of it. Can I just say OH SHIT! LOL

A couple comments on your comments—we are different and I AFFIRM that—can you hear me? And we are strangely and weirdly the same. I treasure that more than life itself. I already know from listening to you that you are a GOOD man, a fine man, a noble man. I knew that in my heart before now. (Did you ever wonder if your birth mother would be a five-

hundred-pound woman living in a trailer with seven kids from four different men, and a heroin addiction?) Laughing—I move from laughter to tears in a moment these days.

I have wondered how I will relate to you—you are a scientist, and a builder of paradigms and concepts—I am a poet and theologian (sorry, it's true) and a builder of ideas. Clearly, we both love to learn. I also love culture and am wide eyed at the flow of life all over the world. We have that in common.

Let me say this about religion (frightening revelations)— "religion" is a struggle for me. But I believe in God because of you. Does that surprise you? I had no choice. I have thought long and hard about whether humans can really have a connection that is beyond memory and wish dreams. I know you have me in you, physically, and I have you in me. (Did you know that when a woman carries a child, she retains that child's cells in her body the rest of her life?) But could I give you strength even from a distance? Did the fact that I am your birth mother mean that you would be, could be, a more amazing person, besides basic gene transfer, etc.? I couldn't be sure, so I had to believe in God. Someone to come between us and carry my heart to you even if you never ever knew it was that. And, you can do with this what you want, but that I have found you, and found you to be so much more amazing than I ever hoped, so sane (I keep using that word, don't I?) means that I will always deeply believe in God. So, there is my religion.

I have hoped that would not be a barrier between you and any of us. (Ben is the most conservative, and frankly, he and I have had plenty of war between us. We have stayed friends through it all, which I consider a victory.)

Steve is trying to find how to be part of this. But really, I would like to exclude everyone and not have all that confusion. It dismays me that I cannot control your connections to everyone—even though in general I don't enjoy control. I am glad to have some hours with you before he is in the conversation. He is a great guy, and not at all stuffy, although he can seem that way when he doesn't know what to do. LOL

> *I know you are not looking for family. So we will have to figure this out.*

> *Mark—you said it exactly right when you said that we are tied to this fate together. And like I said yesterday, at this moment life transcends art. I will live with my anxiety. Someone once told me that some things are WORTH being intensely nervous over. This is one of them.*

> *You are again gracious to me. Thanks Mark.*

In the end, the rendezvous in Calgary and Banff happened with surprisingly little drama. We met on an ordinary early spring morning in the lobby of a Travelodge and walked across the street to Tim Hortons for coffee. Strangely, the first face-to-face moments were unremarkable to me. A little like being introduced to one of your parents' friends. Sharing the car ride from Calgary to Banff was awkward but good and gave us an opportunity to talk—which was all we really wanted or needed. As the day progressed, I came to know that the visit was more for Marilyn than myself. She had been planning these moments, living them out in her imagination since the day I was born. I was okay with that and went along with the program, answering questions both banal and deeply personal as best I could. To be honest, my most vivid recollection from the weekend was that brief conversation I had with the Canadian border guard in the airport, the one which ended with her wishing me "good luck." Something about that interaction continued to make me feel less alone and give me strength.

It reminded me of the larger world outside of this moment, and all the parts of my life that felt like home.

Chapter 16—Aftermath (Mark)

Letter from Mark to Marilyn and Steve, April 29, 2007

Marilyn and Steve,

I hope the presentations and the rest of the weekend went well for you both. I noticed that the Red Wings pulled one out of the fire yesterday, so I know Steve is happy. :)

I made it home without incident and have spent the last day or so talking with Tina and trying to come to terms with things myself (and trying, unsuccessfully, to catch up on sleep!). I also, of course, was welcomed home by an email from your daughter wanting to know how things went. It took me three hours to compose a response to her—one that was written more for me than for her. I have attached an unedited portion of that note below, as I think that it is an honest glimpse of our visit through my eyes—albeit a partial one; the dust is still settling around me. I hope it is insightful for you. I am sure there will be more to write on this event in the coming days, months, and years of our lives, but not today. There is no word or words I can find to capture my overall sense of the last three days, but I think the closest would be "satisfying." Thank you both for that. Thank you for being open, and welcoming, and warm. And thank you for being the good people you are (the 500-lb.-heroin-addict fears are now completely put to rest).

In other news—Tina and I have looked into Memorial Day flights. Are you sure we should stay with you? I don't want to put Rachel out—she will have her kids with her (right?) and hence will have much greater need for "supportive lodgings."

Tina and I would be just fine in hotel or, frankly, anywhere. Just let us know if any arrangements ought to be made.

BTW I think Steve's suggestion that we establish a usable moniker for me is a good one (and it makes me smile that we need to do this because it shows how rare and precious this meeting is—a colloquial name for my relationship to your children does not even exist!). I am still reticent about "bio brother" (although Tina thinks that is perfectly reasonable). I would like to table the suggestion of simply "other brother." Let me know what you think . . . [note: the real me, the goof and wise-ass, came up with several other far more humorous titles as jokes that were unfortunately stricken from the record.]

Mark

Excerpt of Letter from Mark to Rachel, April 29, 2007

My mind is racing, trying to comprehend and interpret all that has happened to me in the last few days. It will take me a couple of days to sift through it all. Overall, my first impression is a contented one. I think this was much harder for your mother than for me (she missed me, but I never knew her—my quest being driven more by curiosity than sense of loss).

BTW—I know I don't need to fill you in on what transpired in detail, because I suspect you captured all that by phone on the fly! :) I laugh, but it is sweet to see how close you and Marilyn are.

[What follows is a work-in-progress interpretation of the last two days for me. It has been challenging for me to write. I have used the writing process as a mechanism to understand things in my own mind (a useful tool). I am still not sure if I will send it.]

I struggled a little to understand how to interact with them. Who are these people to me? This is not a relationship type that I have any prior experience with. In the end, it felt a little like a two-day job interview. I was truthful, but not always genuine. Somewhere inside of me, there was a little boy that was screaming for his "parents" to be proud of him—so I played up what I perceive as my strengths and what I speculated would make them admire me most. And I played down the differences we have because I didn't want to incur judgment or alienation. Carefully chosen anecdotes that showed who I believe I am in a light that I thought they would find pleasing. (I think Marilyn did some of this as well; Steve much less so.)

One of the downsides to this (from my perspective) is that what I perceive as my strengths will never be perfectly aligned with what your parents perceive as strengths. We have quite different belief systems and are distinctly different people (and yet in many ways have closely aligned morals and values—I wonder why that is?). I think what I failed at in this first quick pass was celebrating the differences as much as the similarities. Showing my whole self in balance—the man I am. It took me many years to define and become the man I am. I am comfortable with him and the paths he has chosen. In my heart I feel I am a good person (at least on balance!), and that is enough to make me happy. And intellectually, I know that your parents will accept me however I am—so it is foolish to try and sell them a version of me that is anything but me in my raw and natural state (I have no plans to change, so they should know what they are getting into!). Not to mention that the idea of a sales pitch for myself always makes me feel unclean somehow (boastful and secretive).

And now I have left you with a skewed impression as well. It was far from a whirlwind of deception and bravado. It is just like me to focus on the 3% that did not go the way I wanted rather than the 97% that did (my own worst critic). And I do think that the back-and-forth questioning, with uncharacteristic emotional candor on my part, has built a framework for us to know one another despite the occasional slanted beam (engineering metaphor—sorry). In many ways, I think it was almost required to lay some sort of foundation for this crazy relationship that has no precedence in our lives.

More importantly, I filled in little pieces of my world that I never knew were missing. I made a new connection that is beautiful to me and completes parts of me in a way that words cannot describe. I see my spirit in Marilyn's spirit, and I see my strength in Steve's strength. Even from a distance, I already see parts of you and your brothers in me (frankly, the connection with you is the most enigmatic to me—perhaps that is a girl thing?). To say that I am looking forward to the next encounter with the Elliotts is the understatement of the year!

[end of the difficult part]

Letter from Marilyn to Mark, April 30, 2007

Hi Mark,

We are flying home today—I finally got to a computer to write and thank you for coming to Calgary. I have many thoughts and images in my mind and soul . . .

best moment—seeing you in the Travelodge (I thought I would melt . . . though I tried to be cool)

kindest thing you said— "it'll be okay" (which you said when I first met you, and I so needed to hear that)

best conversation—at the Rose and Crown (thank God for alcohol or the best things would never be said)

sweetest moment for me—hugging you in the hall

loveliest thought—Tina's embrace of your journey and her finding joy in it funniest story—a tie between your dad's eating habits and the leaping clam

what I liked about you best—your kind spirit, your love of the people who are in your life, your creative brilliance, your eyes, your love of nature, your taste in wine (for starters)

For Memorial Day, Cincinnati is the airport we often use, the drive is not bad at all—not too much more than an hour. It is a good choice. The other option is Louisville. Whenever you come is great—we want you to come for as long as is possible and will stop the world for you. And you SHOULD frankly stay with us. Rachel is playing you—it is a game. She is loving this . . . and we want you to stay with us. When the whole tribe is around, we always farm some of them out so this is usual. "The Girls" will stay with us too.

The "other brother"—that makes me smile. You will get a name—we name the one's we love in the Elliott clan. To me, "bio brother" makes you sound like you were made in a lab and that is far from the truth.

I realize we have all our usual fences and boundaries up again . . . I felt them all on Friday morning and so wanted to go back to the night before . . . but even so, let me say a couple things, just because I need to.

I also struggled, inside, much of the time I was with you. Here's the thing—I felt the whole time like you were just beyond my reach. (I think I could have received you at your rawest, not your best. You probably could have received me, too.) I didn't know what this relationship was, is, either. So many longings that couldn't be put into words for me, so much I needed but didn't want my needs to be the priority, and didn't want to violate your choices, postures, personhood. I was sad that it felt like a job interview, but it did, sort of. I thought it was me who needed the job, though. ;-) I was also truthful but not free.

So many times, I thought we were talking about the wrong things but I didn't know how to find my way to the right things.

When we left you at the airport and started to drive north, I cried and cried. My sorrow was on several levels. Having found you I now have a greater loss, a grief of epic proportions for me. (I understand you are on a different journey than me in this—please know this is just trying to tell the truth.) Mark, what I told Steve as I tried to explain my grief to him was that I had encountered a love for you that was greater than I even knew, and yet I feared and felt like we might never find each other because we (might) have such different world views (but they might not be as different as all that). And yet, like you say, our starting points are different but our landing places are so similar. I know I didn't get or give what you describe as "authentic" in every conversation—I knew that, but I did feel that we do have the same spirit, you and I, and there is nothing in what you are or might be that would keep me from enjoying you at every level. But how to move past where we are to authenticity?

I loved your spirit. I so enjoyed everything about you—even with the angst I felt inside. But what the hell—how on earth do you meet someone who is a completely new person and really get to know them in such a short time? And add to that the desperate (at least on my part) longing to be known and loved and welcomed? It was, as we say, a completely forlorn hope at its fullest, but remarkably satisfied, none the less. How far we got is remarkable. You must have been relieved, though, to get back to Tina and the sweet comfort of being in a place where you are fully known . . . there is nothing better than that.

Maybe being with the kids will help us understand each other more. Each one of us is so remarkably different in how we interpret the world for ourselves. I hope you will find it freeing. I am all about consonance—living out the realities of your inner truth (sounds so ethereal)—and you are doing that. You told me bits of how you struggled when you were young . . . and how fierce-ness came to you over time . . . never give that up.

Just as a matter of saying truth, I felt like Steve highlighted all the wrong differences and his views certainly don't represent mine (a long-term reality in our relationship) so you have yet to meet his real self as well.

All that being said, I have to tell you, Mark, that every glimpse you gave me of your inner self was a treasure to my heart. My sense of loss is profound. I thought if and when I ever found you that I would be satisfied, and instead I find that first I have to work through a grief of a loss that is more profound than I could have dreamed. My nights are filled with tears. I don't fully understand this love and this loss. In a sense having found you to be who you are (and maybe I see who you are more than you give me credit—take into account my intuition and mother's heart—formidable foes :-)), I now lose you in a more profound sense.

So, I am left with a mixed sense of richness and sorrow. You are a gift beyond the telling. Whatever happens from here on in—we will discover it by walking. "Solvitur ambulando"— St. Augustine's advice on solving life's riddles— "solved by walking together" is what it means. That I can do. I also look forward to the long weekend with anticipation and joy. Most of all I carry the profound hope that in some way, you will stay in my life.

Now I have used up all my time before we leave and I shall be forced to travel unclean . . . pull my hair into a pony and put on sunglasses and poke my nose into a book.

You are loved. Just as you are. Marilyn

Chapter 17—Meeting Mark (Rachel)

We all wanted to pick Mark and Tina up from the airport, but I put my foot down. With arguments I no longer remember, I was adamant. I was picking them up. All by myself, thank you very much. This was going to be the first time I laid eyes on my big brother, and I was beyond excited!

What to wear?! I didn't want to dress up but didn't want to be too casual. How to wear my hair?

I had told Mark that I didn't want to arrange a meeting place or have him wear "a flower in his lapel," because I was convinced that I would recognize him among the deplaning throng. So I stood, bouncing on my toes, while I waited for him in the designated area at the airport. Behind me I heard an older lady whisper to her companion, "I think she may be excited." I turned to grin at her, and almost spilled the miraculous story of my secret brother, but I held it in, like Mary, treasuring the moment in my heart.

Groups of people started to pass me in clusters, the way they do in airports, and around me *welcome backs* and *good to see yous* were being exclaimed amid hugs and handshakes, but no sign of Mark. I started to worry that maybe I had missed him, that there would be no instant recognition. I craned my neck and stood as high as I could on my sneakered toes, and suddenly, there he was! Taller than the average traveler, his eyes bobbing over the tops of the head of the people in front of him. We made eye contact and I knew. I went flying through all the people in front of me and threw my arms around him. Pulling back, I broke every protocol in the book (I'm sure!) by placing my hands on the sides of his startled face and saying, "You exist!" I didn't care about whether or not he needed personal space, or how he felt about seeing me. I just wanted to touch him and make sure he wasn't a figment of my imagination. After countless emails and years of wondering, my big brother was right there in front of me, and I wanted to absorb him into my life. I could have consumed him right there. My big brother!

Suddenly, I remembered that he was not alone, and I pulled Tina into a quick hug. I laughed and said, "I don't want you to feel left out!" to which she replied, "Oh, I expect a lot of that this weekend." I hope that wasn't her experience, but it probably was. I would change that if I could, but looking back, finding any kind of balance was impossible.

There are so many things I remember about that weekend, but one thing stands out above the rest. I wish I had looked at him more. I arrived home to North Carolina and realized how often I had let my eyes slide away out of shyness—the sudden nearness of him too much for me—and I wished I had looked more. Stared right into his face to make up for years of not looking, not seeing. Not being able to see. I wished I had mapped out the aspects of his face that were familiar, reflecting the faces of my brothers and my dad, and the aspects that were not, the things that were just him. But I was too shy, too nervous, so I didn't.

I have a picture of us at the airport, and even years later, I look at it often. I look at my grin and Mark's smile and, to borrow the words of a much better writer, I think to myself, what a wonderful world.

Chapter 18—Memorial Day (Mark)

Less than a month after the weekend in Calgary we sat together, all of us, for the first time at Marilyn and Steve's home in Nicholasville, Kentucky, just outside of Lexington. Rachel and Curtis had driven up from Durham, North Carolina with their daughters, Meg and Kyra (ages eight and ten), Ben and Kari had flown down from Calgary with their infant son Blaise, and Vincent had driven over in a recently acquired PT Cruiser from his apartment above a liquor store downtown. How he afforded the car I was not quite sure, given that his employment status at the time appeared to be a moving target.

The walls of the home were cleanly painted in various light shades of yellow and white. Appliances were modern but not extravagant. Furnishings were contemporary but not opulent. The room was bright and airy. Everything in the home seemed chosen for comfortable living. We were distributed about the home's great room in haphazard clumps of board gamers, wine drinkers, raconteurs, and sous chefs. To the untrained eye, our gathering there would have seemed a perfectly normal, casual, family affair. The extreme novelty of the moment was pushed down into the subtext of our interactions to allow that semblance of normalcy we all crave in absurd times. For my part, I was quickly learning the game *Settlers of Catan*, and leveraging my position as the guest-of-honor for every advantage I could. The game provided a comfortable distraction, a context for conversation and a device for filling awkward silences in this most unlikely of reunions.

Truthfully, though, silence did not figure prominently in anything that transpired that weekend. As a collective unit, the Elliotts are storytellers and attention seekers. There is a natural unforced loudness to them that would be unnerving if it were angry, but the Elliotts only seem to raise their voices in praise—usually of themselves. There is a theatrical air to their comportment; quick to take cues from one another and feeding off each other's energies. They play favorites, they tease, they agree, they shy from conflict, and they avoid dissonance in favor of welcome, even in the face of legitimate issues. And they do it loud—a brash storm that would be overwhelming to many, including Tina. Navigating the tempest with poise and confidence, Rachel sat at my left at the kitchen table for the game of *Catan*. I often caught her staring at me with a goofy smile on her face, trading me cards with the sort of generosity usually reserved for parents trying to intentionally lose a game to their five-year-old child. Over her shoulder I would occasionally see Tina across the room, reclined on the sofa with a glass of wine in her hand or engaged in polite conversation. I didn't dwell long enough in those moments to determine to whom she was speaking—I was too engrossed with my own affairs to understand or really care about her situation. Alone across the room, she was left to fend for herself against the onslaught of rambunctious new relations—relations whose extraversion was so antithetical to her own quiet ways. Even though they harbored only the best of intentions toward her, it was a lot to ask of anyone, let alone shy and reserved Tina.

Indeed, Tina's struggles with my new world started well before we arrived in Kentucky. They started after the first messages were exchanged, when I would stay up late writing emails to people she didn't know and had no real reason to trust. They started when I had no energy or interest in anything but this new family. They started when she would turn the corner into our home office and find me hurriedly shutting down the computer, embarrassed by how much time I was spending on correspondence with them. I should have paid more attention to how I was acting and how it must have made her feel. Instead, I had spent the previous eight weeks thinking only of myself. By the last week prior to the reunion, I was counting the days until our visit like a kid counting down to the last day of school. I was an absent husband, a selfish ghost in our home and in our marriage.

Single-mindedly focused on my correspondence with the new relations, I sent reams of messages showing only my best sides, cataloging my triumphs and glossing over my shortcomings to project a shining vision of my personal greatness. This, I would learn, was entirely consistent with the Elliott traits of self-aggrandizing and self-praise. I wanted to see myself returning home the conquering hero. And I was so wrapped up in that fairy tale that I was ignoring my true home with Tina, sequestering these new experiences from my true life with her. I was embarrassed by how emotional I had become. The thirty-five-year-old pragmatic husband in me was overthrown by the little boy who wanted to make his mommy proud.

On the Friday of our departure for that Memorial Day reunion, I skipped down the stairs into our foyer and didn't notice the look on Tina's face until I was practically on top of her. She was quaking slightly, standing behind our suitcases by the door, softly crying with her shoulders rolled forward in sad defiance and withdrawal.

"I'm not coming," she said.

I stood frozen, dumbfounded. My first thought, before I even thought to ask why, was for myself: it was the thought of showing up and having to explain to the new family why Tina was not there. My stomach knotted tightly and then tighter still. I heard ringing in my ears and felt blood rushing to my head. My skin began to tingle all over, almost painfully, as it anticipated the panic sweats that were coming. The fragility of my self-made heroic façade was made plain before me. I couldn't show up without Tina, I would be undone; reality can be a horror.

All that burst through my mind before I was even able to consider her feelings. It was only then that saw the truth: in the fervor of my pursuit of knowing the Elliotts, I had turned from Tina. She was hurt, she was jealous, and she was right to be. At that moment, I saw it clearly in the furrow of her brow and tension in her neck. How could I have not noticed earlier? My mind flashed briefly to my parents: it was the second time I'd unintentionally wounded someone I loved, this time my closest partner in life. For Tina, the prospect of immersing herself with these people, the ones for whom her husband was seemingly abandoning her, was simply too much. She needed out.

But I could not allow her escape. I could not bear it. I would not bear it. Selfishly, I mustered my resolve and called upon her to honor our too often unspoken commitment to each other and insisted she come with me. I stood in the hallway, door as yet unopened, with a bag in each hand while I entreated her to reconsider. My heart was filled with sadness and desperation. I promised to be more attentive, more honest, and more careful with her. I coerced and she capitulated—although I'm not sure to this day if it was out of forgiveness or fatigue. She wiped her tears and I set about trying to internally rebuild my ego, vainly hoping to be done before touchdown at Cincinnati International Airport. Tina was wary and uncertain. I was shaken but soldiering on.

So, we went. Rachel had tasked herself with driving to Cincinnati to pick us up and deliver us the last mile. The Cincinnati airport is south of the Ohio River in Kentucky and is the closest major airport to Lexington. She met us with a giddy smile that spread beyond her ears and fierce, engulfing hugs for each of us. From the moment she saw us coming out through security, she was bouncing and waving like a champagne bottle at a victory party. She immediately launched into happily babbling about everything. Seriously, everything. She had thirty-plus years to fill me in on. I did my best to keep up. It was warm and welcoming, and so surprisingly comfortable. Tina sat in the back seat and was quiet for most of the drive. Rachel made several overtures of inclusion during the hour's drive to Marilyn and Steve's home in Nicholasville, and I made one or two myself, but the conversation was dominated by our duet. The reunion had begun.

In the end, I did not need a façade. There was no place in the Elliott home for a conquering hero. There was only a comfortable place on the sofa and an invitation without pressure to join the raucous circus of their weekend. I felt implicitly comfortable among them, reveling in the warm sting of gentle jokes at my expense and returning my own salvos. I had brought my polished resume, but they set it aside, unread. There was no judgment, only togetherness and the constant gregarious din of the Elliott clan. Amid their good-natured goading and button-pushing was a liberal sprinkling of poignant anecdotes as they relived their family highlight reels for me one glimpse at a time.

These sometimes caused me moments of reflection which were both comforting and sad—surreal moments when I looked around the room at the faces about me and considered the seeming impossibility of who these people actually were.

At some point in the weekend Ben disappeared. When I finally noticed and enquired with Marilyn, I got an equivocating response about the challenges he was having processing all this change. Unlike Rachel and Vincent, Marilyn had never confided in him about my existence, about her shameful mistake, at least not until my dramatic reintroduction to the family a few weeks prior. He had had far less time to prepare. While it was understandably a lot for him to reconcile, he never betrayed his struggle when he was present—our interactions were only strong and heartfelt. I did not judge him for retreating, although I got the sense that others may have. Clearly Tina was not the only one struggling with all this turmoil. After talking with Marilyn, I wondered if they had had a conversation similar to the one Tina and I had had at our front door; questioning whether he could muster the will to come. But again, I was no help. I quickly slipped back into Christmas-morning mode—running from present to present, trying to build as many memories as possible, trying to make up for thirty-five years of separation in one weekend. If I didn't have time for Tina, my wife, then I surely didn't have time for Ben. There was simply too much for me to take in. I was a child with fingers in the icing bowl—not thinking about the possibility of a stomachache later on.

The first full day in Kentucky was highlighted by an extravagant dinner. Marilyn had purchased a large prime rib roast of beef, the cost of which was brought up by Steve more than once. They concluded that I was worth it, to be sure, but there are some for whom frugality is not so easily set aside. Plenty of sides were planned to accommodate Tina, the sole vegetarian among us, but I also offered to make some of my signature vegetarian Yorkshire puddings to go with it. This offer provided a trifecta benefits: broadening Tina's dinner menu, showing off my cooking abilities (assuming they came out okay— Yorkshire puddings are notoriously finicky), and providing another safe dinner item for my own picky palate. By happy coincidence, Yorkshire pudding was also an Elliott family favorite, and I was told that its absence was often lamented if a roast was served without the little bread wads. Dinner was pleasant and cheerful, and slathered in gravy—original and vegetarian. The food was good and the Yorkshires were, of course, a big hit. As the guest-of-honor I was excused from the cleanup, although I was pretty sure that I would not be waited-on for long in this crowd.

The weekend was short, and by the end of it I was happily exhausted. New bonds of friendships had been forged and understanding was beginning to form. What struck me most wasn't that there were people in the world that were like me in some ways, but that there was an undeniable, almost tangible, difference in the way I interacted with these people compared to how I had interacted with anybody else in my life. It was like I knew them before I met them. I was an *a priori* insider. I immediately knew how they would react to a given action or comment, not because I knew them as people and could predict their responses, but because I could see myself so strongly in them and project my own reactions onto them. It was wonderfully intimate in a way I hadn't really known before. It felt homey and comforting.

In the weeks that followed, I kept coming back to that feeling of comfort and security. There was an innate value to being in their circle. This is what a biological family must feel like. I had the unexpected realization that I would never want to adopt a child. When this story started, I had assumed that finding and connecting myself to my hereditary roots would appease any misgivings I had regarding my own adoption. I thought it would slake that thirst for connection and make me feel more comfortable raising a child that was not biologically my own. Instead, I discovered the deep intrinsic value of relating to genetic kin.

Now I craved more of that feeling. I wanted for me and Tina to have our own biological children, our own biological family. Tina was still indifferent on adoption versus surrogacy, wary about the expense and challenges associated with either, and especially the seeming impossibility of finding a willing surrogate. But for now, she deferred to me to choose our path. I decided that we would need to find a way to make surrogacy work. As far as I was concerned, it became the only viable option.

It would be years before Tina and I revisited aloud the darker, more painful moments that cast shadows over that weekend. Whether it was out of cowardice or commitment I'm not sure, but we both either ignored or suppressed all thoughts about our relationship's brief visit to the brink. I knew that it had been jarring for her, but at the time, I didn't realize how jarring, I couldn't see how excluded she felt. In much the same way, she didn't understand how exposed and vulnerable I was in that moment, and how much heartache her resistance caused me. We both underestimated how much hurt was wrought. Our lives would be easier if either of us were better at sharing our feelings. Fortunately, as true pragmatists, we also both knew that no life, and no marriage, and no partner is perfect; some struggles we overcome, and some we just try to manage well enough that they don't break us. In that spirit, we continued moving forward, quietly and together, trying our best to not bear grudges.

Chapter 19—Knowing the Elliotts (Mark)

Between the intense visits and the barrage of letters, it did not take long for me to get a sense of the Elliotts for who they were—scratching through the veneer of best-feet-forward and accounting for the shading of my own rose-colored glasses. They were so different from me and yet the same.

The biggest difference was obviously going to be religion. It seemed to me, at least initially, that religion defined them. Steve, my biological father, was a senior pastor in a smaller, nondescript Christian denomination; Marilyn worked at a seminary college in Kentucky. Faith extended thoroughly through my new siblings too: Rachel had married a pastor; Vincent worked, at least part time, in one of the church offices with his dad; and Ben was completing a doctorate in religion and philosophy—it seemed clear that his future career would be somehow connected with the church. It was the color of their skin.

In contrast, I had founded myself on science and reason, pragmatism and analysis. I believed in the truth of nature and a fate governed by the laws of physics. Early on, as I reflected on the Elliott's faith, it occurred to me that I knew next to nothing about how religion actually worked. I knew the Cliff Notes: Adam and Eve, Noah, Jesus and the crucifixion, something about apostles, but little about life as part of a church community. My own mother is Jewish and my father Protestant, both lapsed. At one point, they considered sending me to temple on

Saturday and church on Sunday, but thankfully they settled on neither. I wouldn't say that I completely lack spirituality, but whatever I believe in is agnostic at most, devoid religious dogma, tied only to nature and the universe. The idea of a prescriptive morality dictated by any sort of authoritarian religious construct had always struck me as repugnant. I had grown up seeing organized religion not as a mortar that could hold a community together, but as a source of unnecessary strife in the world, and often as a predication for war.

I worried about whether or not these stark differences between us could be reconciled. Surely, I thought, at some point the question of faith would arise, and it would undo my fledgling relationship with the Elliotts. My impression had always been that disagreement was not well-received by religious people. So I was surprised and admittedly pleased when religion ended up not entering our conversations. They were people. They were smart, well-educated, and good. They read and wrote incessantly and were well-versed in music and the arts. There was no hint of judgment, or preaching, or proselytizing.

I was also caught off guard by how free they were with their love and how easily they voiced their feelings—two arts with which I have always struggled. But getting to know them was easy for me despite my lack of emotional fluency, whether it was the magnitude of our situation that overwhelmed my normal social resistance, or all the innate similarities between us, the process of opening myself up to them was simplified somehow. They were wrapped in vague familiarity. Interacting with them was like revisiting a recurring dream. They were somehow already known, at least in part. Fragments of me were reflected in them, which was both surprising and comforting. And parts of them cast light on portions of myself I had never noticed or tended to, now visible and attainable for the first time. The identity I had forged for myself from childhood, through education, friendship, marriage, and career, grew more in the spring of 2007 than it had in many years.

Marilyn was sweet, tender, and a little broken. I felt that I could not possibly fill the hole she had in her. She would have done better were I still the child she gave up, and not the man I had grown into. I had no childhood left, the man I had become was all I had to offer, and even then, I was only able to give of myself in pieces. Sometime later I shared with Marilyn a collection of pictures from my childhood loaned to me from my mom. The collection was inadvertently sorted in reverse-chronological order. As she flipped carefully through the images, studying and absorbing each one, she smiled and laughed, celebrating my life and my adventures in college, high school, middle school, and continuing on down, until she got to a class portrait of me at about the age of six. At that moment, the happy boy in the story the photos told suddenly connected to the baby she had given up, and she broke. With shaking hands and tears on her face she gripped the photo tightly, as precious as a winning lottery ticket, as fragile as a pressed flower. Part of her clearly wanted or needed to be my mother, but I already had a mother. It is relatively easy to make emotional room for a new sibling; a new parent is an entirely different matter. She wanted to know every moment of my life and history, many of which I had left behind a long time ago, and I just wanted to know who she was now. We still wrote regularly, often connecting deeply, sometimes talking across one another, in either case it felt good.

I only exchanged words with Benjamin a small handful of times. His world was one of conviction and rigor—probably the most similar to mine of any of the Elliott clan, but written in a different tongue. He and I had the same adherence to structure in our views on the world, only he had built his structure upon philosophy and religion, whereas mine was built upon science. Yet, he was mathematical and clear-headed in his own way, also quick witted and a bit of a smart ass, qualities I thoroughly embrace in myself. It was too early to get a complete read on him, I needed more data.

Vincent vacillated between timid and effusive, simultaneously gregarious and shy. I would hear from him in widely spaced bursts, miniature tsunamis of humor, love, and adoration. Interacting with him was a little like waiting around in the cold on February 2nd, wondering whether or not the groundhog would show his face, and if he did, whether he would stay a while this time around or just duck back into his hole. Vincent was an aspiring writer and poet, although I had yet to read any of his writing outside of our personal correspondence. I loved him more than I knew him. He was chasing his dreams with more resolve than planning, and I admired that. I can't go anywhere without a plan. I immediately noticed that we made the same dumb jokes and reveled the same way in our own hilarity. Someday, when life allowed, we would have to come to know each other over beer and pizza—or perhaps a bottle of wine and a nicely grilled steak. Although I suspect he would feel more comfortable with the former.

Steve was enigmatic. Marilyn told me that she had asked him to step back from the process of getting to know me. After going through the experience of my birth feeling so alone, she treated our reunion possessively at times—especially when it came to Steve. That was probably why I had so little real interaction with him in those early months. Although, even without much direct communication, it was clear that he was the undisputed patriarch of the Elliott family. He had built this tribe like a fortress around himself—strong, tightly woven, full of love and ferocity, and to some extent isolated from the dangers of the outside world. Yet here was I, standing at the gate, his defenses powerless before me. My birthright was my free pass, a skeleton key through any door I chose, no matter his locks. I could travel and do completely as I pleased within his walls, without regard for rules or protocols. I could choose to love, connect, explore, and bring new light of my own, or I could run amok and tear the walls down. It must have been hard for him to trust me, an unknown, with such power over his fiefdom. I know it would have been hard for me to extend that kind of faith in his situation. But I learned that Steve is a man of faith as advertised, all kinds of faith, and if he did have fears, he did not betray them. He was warm, but aloof, and dutifully stood back to allow Marilyn to have her fill of me.

Rachel was, by far, the one I communicated with the most. She had grabbed onto me with no intention of letting go, and without thoughts of consequences. We wrote to each other at least once a day. With time, our correspondence grew less scripted and more natural. I loved that. I didn't realize until three months later how much I had underestimated her love and commitment to this new family.

Part 2—Surrogacy

Chapter 20—Planning a Family, Again (Mark)

I checked my watch and peered at the potatoes that were simmering on the stove; almost there. Tina would be home from work soon. The smell of curried honey from the chicken breast baking in the oven was now permeating the whole house. Technically there was also a hunk of tofu curing in the same marinade, but I like to think that the smell was coming from the chicken side of things. Honey-glazed chicken was a recipe I got from my mother—my real, adoptive mother. I had changed it a little over the years to suit my taste, trading off mustard for spice and curry powder, but it still smelled and felt like the comforts of home. The tofu was for Tina. I do the lion's share of the cooking for us. We had made a deal a long time ago that she wouldn't complain about me not being vegetarian so long as I never asked her to prepare the meat. After years of trial and error in the kitchen, I count myself as a sort-of-cook, with a short but still substantial menu of meals I could make that were adequately tasty. One of the most important things I learned in becoming a sort-of-cook was that pretty much anything you could do to chicken you could do to tofu and it would be edible—sort of. This was our dinner routine.

Tina came in, kicked off her shoes, and unwrapped herself from the accoutrements of her commute— backpack to the corner and jacket slung over the plain white newel post. She said hi and made no comment on the honeyed aroma. We are often a pair of few words.

When they do come, words, like the food, mostly come from me. I compulsively fill the quiet with stories, facts, and anecdotes from the day. Our conversations rarely touch on emotional issues, and those tend to be analytical, almost matter-of-fact, with as much brevity as possible. In and out, without ceremony or pretext, often for no other purpose than to codify our feelings into words. Fortunately, we are no better at hiding our feelings than we are at articulating them, so we are usually on the same page before it comes to the conversation. That night's brief foray would be about Rachel and surrogacy, discussed over honey-glazed tofu or chicken, served with sautéed green beans and garlic mashed potatoes.

"You know, it occurred to me that Rachel might be a good candidate for surrogacy," Tina began in a quiet moment, a lull between anecdotes from my work.

"You noticed that too, eh?" I said with a slightly knowing and agreeable smile. "Yeah, by the textbook definition she is just about perfect—early thirties, experienced mother, healthy and fit." I had thought about Rachel's surrogacy qualifications a lot, and her credentials were impeccable. She had two daughters born without complications, a stable home, and a strong support network of friends and giving people from her church. I hadn't allowed myself any hope, but of course I had thought about it, and clearly so had Tina.

"And she doesn't even have a day job, other than being a mom," I continued.

"Does she want to work?"

"Actually, I don't think she is allowed to work. Curtis is here on a religious-worker visa and as his spouse, she doesn't have work authorization." I had thought about this too. "Her kids are eight and ten now and spending more time at school and with friends—if anything I think she might be bored stuck at home sometimes."

"Huh." For Tina, *Huh* is not used as grunt of indifference, rather it is spoken slowly, with emphasis and a descending tone—typically signifying that she was absorbing new information that was interesting to her.

"You know I can never ask her, right? At least not for a long, long time. Years." No matter how perfect a fit she was, there was simply no way that I could risk derailing the process of our reunion, our refamiliation.

"Hrm," more of Tina's tonal vernacular. *I know.*

I cut into my chicken and took a bite. I could feel us both retreating from the conversation and its emotional weight, our brief foray into that uncomfortable realm concluded for now.

"Did you remember to stop by the vet and get more of that stuff for Evie's ear?"

Chapter 21—Surrogacy (Rachel)

Surrogacy. Without warning, that word planted itself in my mind and began to grow. I was a healthy thirty-one-year-old woman, done having my own children. I hated being pregnant, but suddenly it was all I could think about. What if? *What if?* What if I told my husband what I was thinking? What if I told Mark? What if I said out loud that I would carry their child? What if everyone thought I was crazy? What if I *was* crazy? No matter where I went, or what I did, the idea of being their gestational carrier was always with me. I just didn't know how on earth I could reveal such a wild idea to the people around me.

As it turned out, I didn't have to. We were at dinner one night with friends, and the subject of Mark came up, as it often did. People were fascinated by the story I found myself in, and I certainly didn't need much encouragement to carry the conversation.

We were discussing the pros and cons of adoption versus surrogacy when without pause my husband looked at me and said, "As soon as I heard their story, I thought of you. I think surrogacy is the most beautiful gift you could give someone."

I was stunned. Sitting at the dinner table my eyes filled with tears. I couldn't believe it—it was as though a huge burden was lifted from my heart. That was the night we began talking about if and how this crazy, love-filled idea might work.

I feel as though it's important to note here that I am not one of those women who loves being pregnant and loves babies. I kind of hate babies, actually. When my youngest daughter was two, I had a brief pregnancy scare—half an hour brief. I got so worked up that I called my husband at work sobbing, repeating over and over, "I can't be pregnant. I just can't." Needless to say, he came home and found me locked in the bathroom, hiding. Later that day, realizing I wasn't pregnant, I made an appointment with my gynecologist to get a tubal ligation. I was only twenty-three. The doctor was hesitant and told me he didn't generally approve of doing the surgery on someone so young, but I was adamant. God forbid anything should happen to me, some lovely (but moderately plain and definitely dull, I hoped) woman might want to have more of Curtis' children. God forbid something happened to Curtis, there was no way I was having anyone else's baby. Ever.

I am also not the kind of pregnant woman people love to be around. My own pregnancies were marked by giant, swollen, angry, hormonal irrationalities. As far as Curtis was concerned, the only redeeming quality I had when I was pregnant was that I slept—a *lot*—so there were long periods where he was relieved of my presence. *Pregnant Rachel* is one of the things I kept trying to remind him of as we considered the surrogacy, but he always just nodded his head, smiled, and said, "I can deal with that. I've done it before."

Chapter 22—Vincent Visits Portland (Mark)

Vincent was the first to visit us in Oregon, in mid-July of that first year. Just for a weekend. Unfortunately, it rained most of the time that he was here—which is highly atypical for Portland in the summer. We also lost a day because the airline stranded him in Salt Lake City on the trip out—I would later learn that that was *not* atypical of his travel experiences—although apparently he managed to look up an old flame in Salt Lake City and find "comfortable" accommodations for the night. Also not atypical for him. Our visit was too short.

He told me that flying lemurs are neither flying, nor lemurs. "They are more like gliding raccoons," he said. That is what I liked most about him. He taught me something new. Always storytelling. Knowledge laced with humor. But he was not really my brother after all, was he? Well, he sort of was. He was one of the "other" brothers. And he was not like my brother at all.

He looked like me, grinned like me, and joked like me. But he wore his heart on his sleeve—or at least on his pages. I generally keep mine safely secured deep inside. Emotionally speaking, he struck me as reckless. Reckless and brave. And a little scary. I wondered what he thought of me.

When he was here, we didn't really do anything (with a lot of driving). I immediately forgot many of the details of the visit. But he was here and we saw stuff and we chilled. It was awesome. He would not eat the green beans that Tina made. And he didn't warn us that he wouldn't be eating them when he'd had the chance earlier at the grocery store. I know he isn't shy. I think he just kept quiet so that we (Tina and I) would have our first-choice vegetable. Of course, it would not have mattered to us. His first-choice vegetable would have been beer.

I had trouble comprehending how we could be so similar and so different simultaneously. I wanted to be a big brother to him. I wanted to reach out and pick him up. But he was already standing. I wanted to teach him about the world, all the life lessons that every young boy should learn from his big brother, but he was already as worldly as I was—he had already learned those lessons from his other brother, and from his sister, and from his mom, and from his dad, and from living his life into adulthood. How would we become brothers, forming that relationship, without those formative childhood experiences? Initially, I decided that we couldn't, that that chance was lost and the best we could do was complicated friends. That made me sad. Strange that I should be sad about losing something I did not even know existed until a couple of months ago. But in some sense that weekend painted a picture of a lacking that has always been there for me.

My relationship with Neil, my actual brother, had always been fraught with difficulties. I glean from that that while those formative years may be a prerequisite for forming the traditional brotherly relationships portrayed in literature and popular media, they are not necessarily a sufficient condition for developing friendship and trust. And so I did my best to be optimistic. Vincent and I might never completely be brothers. But we could have something brother-like. And we could call each other "brother"—because that part is true, from a certain point of view.

He came for the weekend and I grew to know him a little, and so did Tina. He slept a lot. I used to be able to sleep that way. He ate a lot. I used to be able to eat that way too. He listened to me talk about science, even when it wasn't relevant or particularly interesting for him. He claims he may have come close to losing his leg, tripping over rocks in a dark lava tube we explored under Mount St. Helens that Saturday. Totally worth it.

Chapter 22 addendum (Vincent)

On my first visit to Oregon, I came close to losing my leg, tripping over rocks in a dark lava tube we explored under Mount St. Helens. It was totally worth it.

Chapter 23—Rachel Visits Portland (Rachel)

Curtis had opened the door to surrogacy in May. For three months we let the concept float through our consciousness and conversation, looking for the deal breaker. I repeatedly asked him, "Do you *remember* the last time I was pregnant?" But no matter how many conversations we had, no objection raised itself with which we couldn't cope. On August 16, 2007, I boarded a plane bound for Portland, Oregon to visit my brother on his turf for the first time. And to make the seemingly outrageous offer to be the surrogate for their baby.

It's a *long* flight from North Carolina to Oregon. There are many hours for second guessing. I was anxious about the offer I was about to make. I was worried they'd think I was crazy. I had gone from thinking this would be a good idea to desperately hoping they'd say yes. I was equally terrified they would say yes. As I sat in seat 31D somewhere over Wyoming, my life took on a surreal quality not entirely unlike a made-for-TV special. Girl finds a brother she never knew, meets him, and decides to be the gestational carrier for him and his wife—brought to you by Lifetime. How did this happen to me? I've never led a boring life, but it's always been . . . ordinary. Nothing like *this*.

I spent all weekend trying to decide if *this* was The Moment. I decided not to spring it right off the plane, so it wouldn't consume the whole weekend. I also didn't want to spring it at the last minute, because I figured we would need time for conversations. I mentally set Sunday night, our last dinner, as my deadline. Through the many dog walkings, wine tastings, and meals we shared, I almost brought it up at least three times, but each time my heart would leap into my throat, blocking the words. I began to wonder if I would have the courage to go through with it. I feared they would think I was overstepping my bounds and say no. I was surprised to find that I had reached a place where I didn't know how I would recover if they did.

Finally, Sunday dinner rolled around. I could barely taste my food. The conversation felt stilted and formal to me; I couldn't enter in, couldn't make eye contact. Reaching the point where it was now or never, I took a quick internal inventory and began, "So . . ." My carefully planned speech evaporated from my mind, I was left stumbling over my words. "So . . . Curtis and I had a question . . ."

It was at this point in the evening, just as I had found my courage, that Mark abruptly stood up and left the room because the music had stopped and the dog, Evie, who was laying at my feet, farted rather awfully. I stopped short, and Mark, over his shoulder, called out, "It's ok— keep talking. I can hear you."

Um, no.

I waited awkwardly for him to return to his seat, picking at my plate. He plunked down into the chair and took a big sip of wine. "So, what were you saying?"

"Well," deep breath, "Curtis and I have a question for you. We've been talking about it for a while now, well a couple of months really, and well, we didn't know what you might think of this, but we thought maybe . . ." I couldn't get the words out of my mouth. By this point, both of them had put down their forks, and were looking at me oddly, while I looked everywhere but at them. My eyes began to burn and my throat got thick, but finally I strung the words together. "We were wondering if you'd like us to be the surrogate for your baby." With those words, I finally looked up, needing so much to see that it meant as much to them as it did to me. I had no idea what to expect.

Across the table from me, Tina had her hand over her mouth, covering sudden sobs. Mark sat back in his chair as if pushed by the words, just staring at me, speechless. Tina left the table crying, returning shortly with a box of tissue.

She started nodding, and Mark said, "Seriously?"

I felt immediately relieved; I was weightless. In my mind, when this scenario played out, we had a rational discussion, in which they told me that they would talk it over for a couple of weeks and get back to me. The reality was that it was an instant *yes!* And I confess that their emotional response was reassuring to me. I needed to know that their hearts were in it just as much as mine was. In fact, once the initial rush had settled to the point where we could talk about it, they confessed that they had wondered if one day we would reach a point where they'd be able to ask me if I would consider it, but didn't know if they ever would. They seemed stunned that I would just offer it to them.

Within fifteen minutes, Tina was sitting with a thick folder full of information from their IVF clinic, passing me long lists of blood tests I would need and discussing whether or not I could get in to see their doctor before I left. Talk about not letting grass grow under their feet! Suddenly, things felt a little too much too soon, so I gently suggested that maybe we could just go to the beach as planned, and start with doctors once my vacation had ended, which they happily agreed to.

The rest of the evening surprised me. For the last three months, all I had been able to think about was the idea of this surrogacy. No matter what else was going on, it was always there, sitting quietly at the edges of my mind. Now that it was out there in the open, it was almost like it had so much other space to occupy it left my mind completely. I was free. It didn't even cross my mind until Mark would catch my eye and grin, or at bedtime when I got my first spontaneous hug and another disbelieving *thank you.* I immediately fell into a deep and peaceful sleep, without dreams, without the litany of thoughts that had accompanied me to bed for months. That I felt *more* settled, and not less, was a clear sign to me that I was doing the right thing. There was no agonizing *what have I gotten myself into?* fear. No second guessing. I was *completely* at peace.

Chapter 24—IMetMark (Rachel)

Maybe I was feeling a little bit entitled. After all, I had just offered to have his babies. And besides, I like to think I didn't ask for much when I met Mark. OK, maybe I asked for his undying love, affection, and permanence in my life, but not out loud, not explicitly. I just sort of planted myself in his life and refused to move. In a charming way. It could be that I was still in the honeymoon phase of meeting my Secret Brother, and I figured he couldn't refuse me. Maybe it was the opposite, that I was worried he would slip through my fingers and I would lose him to the ether again. Maybe I just wanted my big brother's approval. One reason or another, there was one ultimatum I gave. One condition to the surrogacy. At some point between August when I made the offer and December when I would travel to Oregon for the implantation, Mark would have to meet My People.

My People. I love them. Mark calls them my Mafia. Curtis and I have lived the majority of my adult life far from home – whole countries away. In lieu of traditional family, we built a friend-family around us. The Girls have never lacked for grownups who loved and doted on them. We've never spent a Thanksgiving or Christmas alone. In fact, the opposite is true. We are always collecting card tables and folding chairs to make sure that everyone will fit. There have always been friends I can count on in a pinch, as reliable as any sibling or parent, some even more so, and I have always tried to be that for them in return. These are my people, and I wanted Mark to meet them. I wanted him to see that my life was beautiful and joyous, crowded with people and love. I wanted my people—who had lived vicariously through our whole, miraculous tale as it unfolded—to meet Mark. It didn't hurt that everyone was asking if they could. I just wanted all the crazy, happy parts of my life to be one giant and glorious whole. I asked Mark if he was able to make the trip. He agreed, and the "IMetMark" party was born.

IMetMark, and the moderate anxiety it produced in me to have Mark in my home for the first time, coincided nicely with the release of the 2007 Beaujolais Nouveau. I headed to my neighborhood Wine Shoppe and purchased two cases (yes, cases) of wine for the night. Everyone was instructed to bring their own glass, and I bought window markers to write names on glasses. (As an aside, this turned out to be a particularly poor choice. It somehow escaped my notice that there are many items made of, or framed behind, glass in my home. And it turns out my lovely, tipsy, and downright drunken friends made good use of the window markers. I would continue to find graffiti in unexpected places for months.)

In retrospect, it was kind of an outrageous demand to insist on his attendance. I made no offer to pay for his flight out, only told him that he had to come meet my friends before the IVF. There is one moment I vaguely remember him asking if I was being serious, and in my giddy, pleased-with-myself state, I laughed and assured him that I was. It was no small feat to make it happen, I'm sure, but he did. He would fly in for less than thirty-six hours to meet my demand. I love him.

Word was spread. Everyone I knew and loved, and a couple more just in case, was invited. I hired a friend with a cleaning business to help me get my house party-ready. I invited my baby brother, Vincent, who was living in KY above my parents' garage, so that Mark would have another face he recognized. I agonized over what my knickknacks said about me, tried to see my home through his eyes. I worried desperately about everything being just right, whatever that meant. I felt surprisingly vulnerable as I paced my clean house, reprimanding my children for breathing and waited for his plane.

Which was delayed. Obviously.

Both of The Boys, Mark and Vincent, arrived within twenty minutes of each other the night before the party, in a whirl of loud and happy chaos. It was so late, and I had gotten wound so tightly waiting for them both that I deflated with contented exhaustion. I kissed both their heads and went to bed, falling asleep to the sounds of cuss words, laughter, and beer caps clinking in the sink.

I am, in my own humble opinion, pretty darn good at throwing parties. There were several things I planned for IMetMark that were designed to draw everyone into the joy that Mark had brought to me. First was a large, blue stork sign in the front yard that declared, "It's a boy!" We filled in his height (in centimeters) and his weight (current, but vanity sized) and date of birth: January 4, 1973. For unto us a Brother is born. Curtis, no slouch in the graphic design field, designed a logo which we put on prize t-shirts and a couple custom t's for Mark, Vincent, myself, and a few other select inner circle members. We had trivia posted throughout the house for guessing Mark miscellanea, and prizes were awarded with great flourish at the end of the night. It was fantastic.

One of the distinct memories I have of that party is stepping back from the interaction and seeing what was going on around me. Nearly 50 people were overflowing the seating and rooms, laughing and talking. Engaging Mark and totally open to him, probably overwhelming him, truth be told, but inviting him to be a part of their lives too, in however small a way. It would be easy to dismiss that as an exaggeration or idealization, but flash forward to nine or ten months later, and it was those same people, my Mafia, who brought meal after meal out to Mark and Tina in Raleigh while they waited for the twins to be old enough to fly. It was those IMetMark-ers who came out to set up the rental house with fresh linens and food for the pantry, offering any help they could to ease the transition into parenthood. They are good people, my people. I love them, too.

Maybe that's what I wanted all along. To have all the people I loved in one place. That night is one of my Top Five Memories of All Time. We all drank entirely too much, and stayed up entirely too long. Curtis, who did have to lead worship at church the next morning, eventually tried to go to bed around 11:30 p.m., but the party was still going strong and he spent several hours wishing for earplugs, I'm sure. When everyone finally left, Mark, Vincent, and I poured ourselves the last remaining splashes of the various nearly empty wine bottles strewn around the house and collapsed into the cushions of the couch. The first sips of our last glasses were taken in smiling silence as we looked at each other and the mess around us. I don't remember our conversation at all, but I remember the feelings. Happy. Connected. Content. I remember looking at The Boys and being overwhelmed with a similar sensation to the one I had when my second daughter was born. I was lying in the hospital bed, holding her while Kyra crawled up for a closer look and Curtis perched on the edge holding Meg's tiny hand. I suddenly knew that I was looking at my whole family. We were complete. That's how I felt, sitting in a half-stupor on the couch that night. I Met Mark. I had my whole family. I felt complete.

Chapter 25—Needles (Mark)

Aside from fertility specialists and a small number of related medical professionals, most people don't often talk or even think about surrogacy. If they do, the conversation is typically dominated by the philosophical or emotional considerations that surround the surrogacy decision itself, a conversation often rife with political or religious subtext. Nobody talks about the mechanics of embryo implantation—at least not until they are actually faced with it—which few such philosophers are. But we now faced exactly that and quickly discovered that what we had taken for granted in our minds as a simple visit to the clinic was in reality a three-month steeplechase of preparations, injections, and regimented medical oversight. Surrogacy seems deceptively simple, if not obvious, when explained in lay terms: (1) collect egg from her, (2) collect sperm from him, (3) mix them together, possibly in a petri dish, (4) put the resulting fertilized egg into the *other her*, (5) bake for nine months—easy-peasy. Even Tina and I, after having wrestled with the possibility of surrogacy for more than half a decade, had never really considered the true mechanics of the procedure. Our question for the doctors had always been, *is it possible?* not, *what's involved?*

Surrogacy, of course, is not as simple as it sounds. Surrogacy is not easy for any of the people involved. Well, for the man, the future father, surrogacy is easy. For him, surrogacy is five awkward minutes in a small white room with an over-played DVD, a small, sterile sample container, and a disposable seat cover. For a man, the process of extracting viable genetic material is old hat. We have had plenty of practice.

The process for the women is not nearly so straightforward. It involves careful planning, expert timing, and a laundry list of medications and supplements: hormones, stimulants, vitamins, and so on. Literally thousands of dollars' worth. For the women, there are no DVDs, only needles. Needles. A barrage of needles. A panoply of needles. A porcupine of needles. Needles every day for more than a month—for both the egg donor (Tina) and the surrogate (Rachel), often more than one a day.

For Rachel, the bulk of the injections given were to synchronize her menstrual cycle with Tina's and to build a healthy and robust womb environment for the future resident(s). Then several more injections were given after the egg-transfer to increase the likelihood of successful implantation and therefore pregnancy.

For Tina, injections were given not just to synchronize her cycle with Rachel's, but also to completely overwhelm it. Interesting fact: not every egg is viable after fertilization in a lab environment. So, because one doesn't want to go through this process more than once unless absolutely necessary, drugs and hormones are used in the critical last month to fool the ovaries into releasing twelve to fifteen of their precious eggs rather than just the usual one. In the days leading up to the extraction procedure, each ovary swells up with a cluster of eggs and start to resemble a miniature bunch of grapes—a miniature yet still uncomfortably large bunch of grapes. Tina had lost a twisted ovary in her early twenties, and so we had just one healthy grape bunch to work with and would be getting considerably fewer eggs. To maximize the odds of success, the doctors would be fertilizing all the harvested eggs and hoping that at least one started to grow vigorously in the lab. Only the strongest growing candidates would have any chance for a successful implantation.

On the last night before the extraction procedure, long after bedtime, a final shot is given precisely twelve hours prior to extraction. This shot is the *everybody-off-the-bus* notice and impels the ovaries to start releasing their precious cargo. This last shot is the one I remember most clearly. It is etched into my memory because it was the only one I had to administer myself. Giving needles is not my thing. The everybody-off-the-bus shot needs to be given in the backside, deep in the meaty muscle tissues where it could most quickly and effectively be absorbed into the bloodstream. Her own backside being a hard place to reach, and the shot needing to be delivered in the middle of the night, the responsibility of giving Tina's final shot fell to her faithful husband at home, me. It is worth noting that this particular needle was three times the size of the previous needles, long and menacing; made to penetrate deep into the layers of muscle.

Tina did not like the look of it at all and was understandably not optimistic about how this injection would feel. Her trepidation was doubly justified by the ever-present shaking of my hands. When I say "ever-present," I really mean "ever-present." My hands have shaken moderately my entire life. This unsteadiness was another genetic trait that I shared with Benjamin and Vincent and other Elliotts on up the family tree— something called intention tremor, or essential tremor. It sounds serious, but it really just boils down to having shaky hands. The harder I concentrate on not shaking, the more pronounced the shakiness becomes. Usually, the worst consequences I have to deal with are messy handwriting and occasional questions from people asking if I'm nervous. It's always been more of an inconvenience than an incapacitation. Now, for the first time in our lives together, Tina was quite concerned about it. My shaky hands were about to stick her in the butt cheek with a harpoon. She was, let's say, "reticent."

Describing this final injection as a painful debacle would be generous. Poor Tina's backside. Poor me. Poor cats, perched nervously at the edges of our bedroom, eyeing us suspiciously as the drama unfolded. I really did try to be brave. It was the middle of the night and we were both tired, but also anxious and excited about the momentous day ahead. As I plunged the needle in, it jiggled and danced in my unsteady hands, gouging and tearing into her tender butt-flesh like an angry rodent. It stayed in at least three times as long as needed to, and, I'm sure, easily hurt six times as much as it should have. But in the end, it was over. The last shot done. Everybody off the bus!

In truth, the only one it was over for was me—Tina still had the extraction procedure to look forward to the following day. But that was tomorrow's problem, and we shared a sigh of relief while I put a Band-Aid over the small puncture wound I left in her butt cheek, and a hopeful, relaxed sleep took us over.

In the end, we harvested a total of nine eggs. Nine single-celled possibilities had gotten off the bus when asked. Tina's remaining ovary had performed admirably. All nine eggs were fertilized via intracytoplasmic sperm injection (ICSI), where healthy individual sperms were selected at random and injected into each individual egg, presumably by doctors, and presumably using all the various sophisticated tools and expertise available at the clinic. We got the growth report three days later. We were good with reports. Reports helped transition the emotional rollercoaster of this experience into an analytical numbers game, something much closer to our comfort-zone. Of the nine, seven fertilized eggs were showing at least some signs of growth. Seven of nine seemed like a good start. Four of those seven were growing robustly—cells dividing and multiplying at normal rates. These four were identified as the "viable implantation candidates." Right now, they were just small clusters of dividing cells, yet each of those little clumps was a possible future person.

The doctors had told us that the typical success rate for an implantation in circumstances similar to ours was about 50%, and their recommended plan of action would be to implant two viable eggs. We decided to follow their guidance; implanting more than two eggs at a time created a significant possibility of triplets, which would be a dangerously high-risk pregnancy for the babies as well as the surrogate. Two implanted eggs would give us roughly a 75% chance of successfully initiating a pregnancy with at least one fetus, including a 25% chance of twins, and a 25% chance of failure. The remaining two viable eggs could be put into cold storage so that we might try again if the first attempt was unsuccessful. The remaining five, the non-starters and the non-vigorous growers, would be scrapped. That was the word the doctors used: "scrapped." It was an intense and loaded word. But in the rush of hope focused on the impending pregnancy, there was no emotional space for qualms about the elimination of the non-viable genetic material samples. It was merely fallout.

The seeds had been harvested. Now it was time to plant. The rest would be up to Rachel.

Chapter 26—The Morning Of (Rachel)

The early December morning of Tina's egg extraction was cold. Even with the scarf I'd borrowed from Mark, I shivered uncontrollably. It may have been nerves causing me to shake, but I prefer to think it was the cold. The three of us piled into the Prius, and it was impossible to read the mood in the car. We were each nervous, scared, excited, anxious, and giddy in turn. Normal conversation was impossible, so I spent the drive looking out the window but barely seeing.

There was no need for me to be there, my debut would be in three to five days, depending on the embryo growth, but Mark and I had plans to wander downtown after the appointment. So, he dropped me off at a coffee shop across from the clinic to wait. I walked in, immediately comforted by the warm air wrapping around me and the aroma of ground beans and sugar. I felt the tension start to drain from me as the warmth seeped in, but a second look around the shop disoriented me. I was suddenly hyper aware that what I was doing, what we were doing, wasn't normal. That it could actually be life or death. Already was life or death. I watched the yoga moms in klatched conversation and hipsters typing away on their silver Macs and felt myself become alien. I didn't belong in this warm coffee shop with its everyday goings-on. I was displaced within myself. That sense of discomfort clung to me while I ordered my coffee to go, and it wasn't until I stepped back into the bracing cold that I began to breathe easier.

Despite the cold, I sat at a table on the sidewalk, contemplating the red brick office building across from me where I knew Mark and Tina were. I prayed for them. I prayed for the little lives that were about to be brought into being. I started to feel my shoulders relax and my heartbeat slow. The pressure and anxiety began to give way again to excitement. Sparrows on the curb picked at invisible crumbs as the pedestrians strode by, full of purpose. Pink, orange, and purple began to overwhelm the gray, early morning sky. Coffee steamed in my hands and I began to hum "His Eye Is on the Sparrow" under my breath . . . "I know He watches me" . . . suddenly feeling rich with love and life.

At that moment, a sparrow heedlessly hurled itself against the glass door of the coffee shop, broke its neck, and died right in front of my eyes. A man, walking out of the shop, almost stepped on it and didn't even notice. Immediately, I burst into tears. Sobbing, I left my cup and crouched over its tiny form, still warm and downy soft. I was not going to let it lie on the cobblestone to be kicked or crushed. With as much tenderness as I could muster, I cradled the body and laid it on the ground underneath the bushes beside the door. Not a single person paid me any mind at all. A sobbing girl on the sidewalks of Portland is maybe not such a big deal.

Retrieving my coffee and turning my back on the sparrow and the clinic, all my withheld and controlled emotions welled up, refusing to be contained. Tears dripped down my face and I didn't even try to hold back the hiccupping sobs as I practically ran away from the clinic. Ahead of me rose an old stone tower topped with a cross, and I headed straight for it. I knew I would find solace in a church. I took a deep breath to calm myself as my hands gripped the cold metal handle of the door. It was locked. Frantically, I looked for another entrance. A wrought iron gate surrounded a beautiful courtyard with benches and fountains—a garden clearly designed to be a refuge. Locked. I leaned up against the black metal bars and cried and cried. I felt so isolated, so lonely. Not even able to find comfort in the familiar surroundings of a sanctuary, I realized how alone I was. Curtis was in NC with the girls and my mom, preparing for Christmas without me. Mark and Tina were dealing with their own experiences, and I didn't want to make them carry the burden of my fear along with theirs. And the three-hour time difference made calling a friend nearly impossible. I'm not sure how long I sat there, alone, but I knew I had to be back at the coffee shop by the time Mark and Tina were done, or I'd miss them.

Nose dripping, I dried my face with the borrowed scarf and dumped my now cold coffee into the grass. I turned around and walked back to the corner just in time to see Mark crossing the street to come find me, their appointment being done. It was both a relief and terrifying to see him at that moment. I was no longer alone, but suddenly everything was very, very real. It was still what I wanted to do, but that was the moment that the gravity of our choices sunk into me.

I smiled a wobbly smile, which he returned with a wobbly one of his own, and we walked back into the warm embrace of the coffee shop together with nothing but hope ahead of us.

Chapter 27—Alone and Together (Rachel)

The room is so dark it is almost black. From where I lay, I can't make out its edges. Of course, that could be the drugs. The barest light falls from a picture unchanging on the screen high on the wall: two small grey circles against a slightly lighter shade. All our hopes pinned to the ceiling. The dimness was meant to soothe and calm, but the effect is undone by the sharp, white light aimed between my knees. I examine my feet, really the only thing I can see clearly, and am glad I chose to wear my knee-high socks. The thick black and white stripes running up my calf are the only protection I have in this room full of strangers and half-strangers. The Valium, like the lighting, is also intended to relax me, which it does—I certainly feel no anxiety—but it has the unintended side effect of making me chatty.

I've never cared much for hopelessness, so I hoped. I knew, inside where knowing doesn't have to be backed up by facts, where hope and love live a happily married life, I *knew*. It was easier for me, I suppose, because those orbs weren't my little life-hopes. I suspect that Mark and Tina were terrified by my cheerful patter, scared not just of hoping, but of pinning their hopes on a loopy girl in wicked-witch-of-the-west socks who had come into their lives mere months before. A girl they barely knew, but who had staked her claim to them and wouldn't let go. Indeed, I had pitched my tent in the garden of their lives like a hippie, wandering barefoot through a history that ought to have been shared. Making up for lost time with ferocity. I knew no other way to be.

So there I lay, naked but for a sheet and socks, feet high in cold metal stirrups, awkward but in awe. In awe of finding Mark. In awe of what intelligence and creativity and persistence have allowed humanity to discover and learn. In awe that I was participating in such a reckless, lovely scheme.

The whole thing took only seconds. Two little futures, resting now in my body. I welcomed them, patted my belly and told them to dig in and make themselves at home, temporary though it would be.

Back in the brightly lit recovery room (what was I meant to be recovering from?) it was just Mark and me, Tina having wiped her tears and left for work. He leaned forward with his iPhone and played me a song that I had previously told him was going to be my theme song for the next nine months. Colbie Caillat. I was suddenly embarrassed, couldn't meet his eye. Maybe the Valium was wearing off, but the words dried up and I could think of nothing to say that would fit the moment. It was too big for me.

We drove home mostly silent, Mark and me. I pretty quickly fell asleep on the couch, drained by the emotion of the morning and encouraged by the doctor's orders to spend three days laying down. When I woke up, Mark was on the sectional beside me watching TV and on the coffee table, right in my sight line, was an apple and a knife. It seems like a small thing, but it wasn't. Not to me. Everything we didn't or couldn't say was in that apple. The whole world in a tight, red skin.

I said, "Thanks," and he smiled. It was enough.

Chapter 28—Naked (Rachel)

I was naked when I found out I was pregnant. That seems appropriate, doesn't it? Nakedness is vulnerability, and I was a very vulnerable woman right at that moment. Shot full of hormones, still reeling from the newness of Mark, the craziness of the surrogacy, and full of a desperate fear that the implantation hadn't worked and the tiny lives inside of me had died. They were always lives to me, never eggs or fetuses, always whole, tiny people, and the thought of their not Being anymore was too raw for me to contemplate.

None of us had considered the logistical implications of a Christmas implantation. The limited access to doctor's appointments, for instance. Trying to get in to have my blood drawn for the pregnancy test was next to impossible, and when I was told that it would be after Christmas before the results would be back, I burst into tears. I'm really not a crier by nature, but I was so overwhelmed with responsibility. Mark and Tina had waited long enough for the news of their babies, and I couldn't shake the feeling that it was my fault that it was Christmas holidays and the offices would be closed.

Late in the day on December 23rd I called the clinic in a fit of optimism, but my results were not back yet. They weren't supposed to be, I was reminded. In my heart I believed I was pregnant, but in my head I was terrified that I wasn't, that it was all for naught. The lab technician I spoke to heard the hitch in my voice and took pity on me. He reluctantly told me that he would do the best that he could to push my results through, but I considered it an empty promise from a guy headed home for the holidays.

So I found myself with a headful of shampoo when the phone rang on Christmas Eve afternoon. I was getting ready for our evening church service but had brought the phone into our tiny en suite shower, just in case. Curtis was already gone, and if he had forgotten anything (a regular occurrence) I expected he would call me to help cover the bases. I wasn't even surprised when the phone rang; I just hung my sudsy head out of the curtain and grabbed it, dripping wet.

"Yup?"

"Yes, is this Mrs. Mulder?"

With my elbow I reached over and nudged the water off at the unfamiliar voice. "Yes?"

"This is Duke Fertility Clinic calling with your test results."

"Seriously?" I stepped heedlessly onto the bathmat.

"Yes, we just wanted to let you know that the results of your blood test are back and you are pregnant. Your HGH levels are over a thousand, which is unusually high, but it may have to do with the hormone shots you are taking. I know you were anxious to know before the holidays, and calling you is the last thing I'm doing before heading home today. Congratulations!"

There was a distinct tone of goodbye in his voice, and I struggled past the lump in my throat to croak out, "Wait—super high HGH? Does that mean it's twins? Does that mean that both babies survived?"

"Only an ultrasound can tell us that, Mrs. Mulder, but with levels this high this early in the pregnancy, I wouldn't be surprised. Have a good Christmas." And with that he hung up.

I stood, stunned, dripping, holding the phone in front of my face.

I hollered for my beautiful girls, who were getting fancy in their rooms for Christmas Eve. "Girls! Girls! I'm pregnant! The babies are alive!" They came racing and whirling into the bathroom wide-eyed; the three of us celebrated this crazy miracle, completely unphased by my nakedness. Without thinking I called my mom.

"Mom! I'm pregnant!" I had never expected to say those words again and saying them out loud to her was surreal. I didn't answer any of her spluttered questions or exclamations, though, because I suddenly realized that I need to call Mark and Tina. I think, in fact, I very nearly hung up on her.

With shaking fingers, I dialed the phone. I sat naked on the toilet seat while the girls returned to their rooms. I half-heartedly pulled the towel off the rack to cover my shoulders but ignored the large blobs of shampoo plopping onto the floor. There are some conversations in life I remember so clearly, and some I wish I remembered. This one I don't remember at all, but I remember how I felt. Mark felt so close, right through the phone. I felt so light, so joyful. I was so relieved that we had survived the first hurdle, that everyone had survived the trickiest part. And I felt sure. So sure. Sure that this would be the first of many miracles. Sure that the rest would be a cakewalk. Sure that Christmas is the best time to find out you're pregnant with your brother's babies. And Love. So much Love. For my own girls, chattering back and forth across the hall excitedly about their pregnant mother. For my husband, who loved me enough to let me love outside of the box. For the wee babies in my belly, already growing and becoming the fullness of the women they would be. And love for Mark and Tina, who trusted me with this amazing responsibility.

It was really they who were vulnerable that night. They stood on the other side of the country hoping huge hopes and pinning them on me. I knew where I was and how careful I was being with my health and the pregnancy, but they didn't. How remarkable. People are generally awed at my offer of surrogacy, but I'm awed at Mark and Tina, and their act of faith and hope. An unknown future hanging on an unknown past that was only beginning to be woven into the present. They were amazing. And as I look back on that night, on how I felt, shivering in the bathroom, all I remember is gratitude. Gratitude for their trust and their love, as limited and untested as it was. The three of us, vulnerable together.

I eventually got dressed and went to church. I sang "Angels We Have Heard on High" and "Silent Night." It was a Christmas miracle.

Chapter 29—Twins! (Mark)

When I was eight or nine years old, my parents gave me the best Christmas present of my childhood. It was Luke Skywalker's X-Wing Starfighter, complete with a retractable front landing gear; you could press down on R2-D2's head and make the wings open into the X-Wing attack position. There was even a hidden button on the back that lit up a small red LED in the nose of the fighter, although everybody knows the X-Wing's lasers really came from the blaster cannons at the tips of the wings. I had watched the movies more times than any reasonable parent could deem necessary, and I loved that little Starfighter. Together we flew hundreds of daring missions. The joy that Christmas present brought was nothing compared to the gift that came to us early in 2008. It turns out that there are some things in life to which even saving the galaxy pales in comparison.

In the first week of January, at Rachel's first ultrasound, we learned that both of the implanted eggs had taken root and were growing with vigor. Twins. We were on track to have twins. My future snapped into focus with images of now two children filling out our quiet Oregon home with energy and color and noise and love. *Twins.* Not just a child, but a full family in one quick step, no practice, no warmup. For less than a moment I panicked, then reality wrapped warm arms around me and assured me that I could handle it. Probably. We were having *twins.*

All the greatest gifts come with tradeoffs. Between it being a surrogacy and now multiples, the pregnancy was now considered "high risk." "High risk" is scary language in a doctor's office. Especially at the OB-GYN, where we first truly learn to care more for another life than our own. Tina, Rachel, and I, adjusted again, on the fly, and had to be that much more careful, that much more watchful. Thus came the litany of appointments, tests, needles, peering doctors, comforting nurses, probes, questions, rubber gloves, ID badges hanging from lanyards, and ultrasounds that would continue for the full measure of the pregnancy. For the most part, these could each be planned for, scheduled, and dealt with one by one in a calculable way. And although Tina and I would strive to be helpful and supportive in each and every way we could find, Rachel would ultimately be absorbing the brunt of it. We put our faith in her strength—it was really our only choice in the matter. She committed unflinchingly, and that gave us a place upon which to fix our hope and anchor our sanity.

In the weeks and months that followed, we spent as much time as we could with Rachel, which was, in the end, not all that much. Durham was more than 2,500 miles away, and there were no direct flights. Money was limited; vacation time was limited; and frequent flier miles were spent much faster than they could accrue. We ended up visiting each other about once every three weeks. In the early months, Rachel took turns with Tina and I, enduring the tedium and discomfort of air travel, but as the pregnancy progressed, Tina and I took the burden upon ourselves exclusively—sometimes together, sometimes just me.

We developed relationships with doctors in both cities. Familiar staff and nurses would smile as Rachel strapped in for her monthly poking and prodding. The frequent visits were so uneventful that they bordered on the mundane, save for the brief, grainy, ultrasound glimpse of the twins we got at the culmination of each appointment. The main challenge seemed to be the sheer number of people in the room, the clinics were simply not sized for our surrogate experience—a pregnant woman, her husband, and the two parents of the babies, along with a nurse and an ultrasound tech all cluttered into a ten-by twelve-foot room already half-filled with diagnostic equipment that was beeping and booping as much as R2-D2 in the back seat of Luke's Starfighter. I lost track of how many times we had to explain our situation. It made for consistently awkward small talk. I suppose there was no casual way in 2008 to say, "That's my pregnant sister who is carrying my twins, and this is her husband, the pastor, and oh yeah, here is Tina, the mom, so yes, we all need to be here. Sorry it's so crowded." But our plethoric attendance wasn't the only irregularity the staff had to work around, they also had to recalibrate all of their well-practiced commentary—each nurse's words of support would struggle to accommodate our situation. They would pause for a moment, considering which woman to congratulate or which to empathize with, and in moments of silence, none would speak a word, for fear of saying the wrong thing. For fear of hurting Tina. It is only as I reflect back on those moments, years later, that I see how unrelenting and alienating it must have felt for her. The qualifications and explanations and veiled judgements— both meant and unmeant—each painted over with polite, supportive banalities. The truth is, I don't really know how it made Tina feel to be such an outsider to her own pregnancy. I never really asked. At that time, between trying to be as supportive as I could to both Tina and Rachel, trying to stay on top of the logistics of the whole thing, and dealing with the emotions of my adoptive reunion, I couldn't bring myself to try and buttress Tina's foundations the way a husband ought to. Tina, I'm sorry that I didn't do better.

As difficult as those awkward moments were, it was incredible to watch our twins grow and develop in Rachel's womb. Each new ultrasound showed a little more detail; gave us a little more information on the miraculous development of tiny people from those two microscopic lumps of undifferentiated cells implanted back in December. Two girls, we were told. Twins. Twin girls. We could see, over time, how the two very different girls settled into their respective roles within the womb. One was particularly active—stretched out horizontally across the top, feet unfortunately kicking Rachel's liver on a regular basis. The second was just the opposite—sitting right side up (breach) in the lotus position, as if meditating. Nearly a decade later, the kicker, Aly, reminded Rachel of her discomfort with a joke text that read: "liver, liver, liver, liver, *pancreas*," which made her laugh out loud, and made me proud to be the parent of a nine-year-old that could spell "pancreas" correctly. Zoe, the meditator, laughed too, but she laughed at anything in those days.

Back in 2008, supporting Rachel from the opposite side of the continent was a challenge, but for me it was a continuation of my genetic reconnection, so I enthusiastically did more than my fair share of the travel. That was when I really got to know Rachel. Relaxing with her family on a Saturday afternoon was so wonderfully intimate. Playing board games in the evening was peaceful, welcoming, and boisterous. Late morning Sunday coffee remembrances of childhood experiences were touching and informing. These moments seemed to transcend our many years apart and I came to know

Rachel for the spirited, tangible woman and mother she is, as well as the spirited child she once was.

Curtis and Rachel's spare room, her own daughters' playroom, with toys and craft supplies lining the walls, filling the closet, and peeking out from under the bed, became my surrogate bedroom in the final months. Her girls didn't really mind, or at least they didn't show it. They were enjoying their mother's pregnancy as they might an entertaining TV show playing in the background at a party. It was going on, they were interested and intermittently engaged, but they didn't seem to take it too seriously. I loved getting to know them too.

Rachel's husband Curtis gave constant and steady support to her and to us. Generous and good, Curtis was a pastor and music director at a modest local Christian church, and the sole bread winner for the family. We knew that he would face significant burdens as well as some public awkwardness because of the surrogacy, and he definitely did. It was not just the strain of the pregnancy on their family unit, but the strain from our story: it could not have been easy for him to explain to his friends and church community that while his wife was, in fact, pregnant, he was not the father. No explanation could be simple or brief, or even comprehensible to some. The revelation that his wife had only recently discovered a long-lost brother, and she was somehow now carrying a child for this brother and his wife was stunning. There must have been those that did not or would not understand. There must have been whispers in far corners of every room. There must have been those who doubted him. I say "must" because this is all assumption and conjecture on my part, as again, I didn't ask. Curtis remained implacably jovial and loving throughout. His support was Herculean. That is another debt I can never truly repay.

We did our best to support Rachel and her family in every way we could think of and with all the resources we could muster. We paid for babysitters and pregnancy massages. I even gave up alcohol, speaking of Herculean support, in solidarity with Rachel, who has been known to enjoy a glass of wine after a long day but now couldn't. It is my understanding that during that time Vincent, faithful brother that he was, graciously picked up the slack for both us—anything for family. We bought Curtis a big screen TV to watch hockey on—at least as much an apology as a thank you. But as much as we leaned in, it was her own network of friends and community that really got her through the pregnancy. They rallied to her in a way that was foreign to me. I loved to see it, and to get to know them a little. I felt happy for her life. Happy for my sister, and for the life she had built around herself, not just the life she was nurturing within her womb.

Winter and spring of 2008 were the hardest, best, and most expensive seasons of my life. As we all juggled supporting each other through the hard parts, there were times when I wasn't sure if I could keep all the pieces together. In those moments, it was Tina's strength from which I drew my support. Tina, the expectant mother forced from the spotlight by so many circumstances beyond her control, somehow managed to maintain her quiet and capable composure by doubling down on her levelheaded pragmatism. She kept our plans in order, kept our bills paid, and kept me going. More than that, her reserved sanity amid the tumult of the Elliotts left open a window for me into my prior life, reminding me of who I was, my natural and original self, as I worked on understanding that the Elliotts were a real part of me too.

Chapter 30—Pregnancy (Rachel)

Surrogacy is hard. I agree. But it also has a weird rock star element. Suddenly every stranger I ran into had the potential to be paparazzi, wanting a piece of me and my story. It usually began with some lovely southern grandmother smiling widely at my daughters, asking them if they were excited to be big sisters. This happened a lot at the grocery store. My instinct, and what I tried to do, was smile, nod, and move on with deciding whether I was craving smooth or crunchy peanut butter. But Kyra and Meg had picked up on the glimmer of celebrity and clamored to be the first one to burst out with, "My mom is having her brother's babies!" Of course, you can't just let that go without some kind of clarification. The inevitable head-swivel and immediate facial transformation from pleased to appalled on grandma's face couldn't really be ignored.

So it was that I would find myself in the cereal aisle trying to explain about Mark, about the surrogacy, about the twins. When people heard what I was doing they were always amazed. A barrage of questions usually followed my prepared statement—people always wanted to hear the details. At first, I must admit I was both flattered and proud, not to mention that I loved to tell the story. Talking about it made it more real, more concrete. You would think that being pregnant would be concrete enough, but somehow it just continued to seem surreal. Saying the words made a difference—I'm not sure how else to explain it. Eventually though, after the umpteenth time at the store or the pool, it just got to be too much.

And so, the day came when I actively taught my beautiful, innocent daughters to lie.

After years of requiring honesty and teaching them the value of the truth, I found myself in the amusing position of explaining to my eight- and ten-year-old girls that we were going to lie about my pregnancy to people— a lot of people. Not our friends, of course, not the people at church, but the random people, the grocery store people, the kind strangers who took one look at my twin-sized belly and exclaimed, "Oh my!"

Our conversation happened in the car one summer afternoon, after the Kroger bags were loaded in and everyone was buckled up. I twisted my swollen self toward the back seat and explained that while all of this was very exciting, we didn't need to tell *everyone* all the nitty-gritty details. I told them that when they were asked the common questions, "Are you excited to be a big sister?" or "Are you going to help your mom?" they should just smile and say, "Yes." It wasn't lying, exactly, I told them. They were excited, and they were helpful; there was just no need to go into the whole song and dance about my secret brother and the surrogacy with every passing stranger who was charmed by the giant belly and the brown-eyed girls that accompanied it. So, we would smile and nod and walk away. The deal was struck.

At first, it worked pretty well; notwithstanding the small question of what we would say after the twins were born and happily ensconced with their parents in Oregon when we returned to the store or the pool without two little babies. I decided we could cross that bridge when we came to it. But still, it worked pretty well until I realized I had unleashed a tiny, angelic monster. Kyra, it turned out, was a champion liar. She couldn't just leave it at smiling, nodding, and walking away. She became a storyteller, weaving absolutely believable and totally untrue tales for the happy grandmothers. The more practice she got, the more detailed her stories became. I can't count the number of times I would paddle over to her at the pool to hear her deep in conversation with someone about how she was taking babysitting classes and was helping me paint the nursery. Or I'd have to drag her away from the nice lady at the checkout line because she wouldn't stop adding elaborate details about how hard it was to choose baby names and our plans for the brothers she was having. She spun more lies than I would have ever thought her sweet little self could come up with. I'm still not sure how I feel about that, but she has grown to be a smart, successful young woman, so I can only assume the damage was minimal?

Chapter 31—Surrogacy and The Law: An Aside (Mark)

Alas, the subject of surrogacy cannot be broached without at least a passing discussion of the legal aspects—arcane, expensive, and often impenetrable. To be clear, I am a firm believer in both the rule of law and that a properly codified social contract is the hallmark of a civilized nation in general. That being said, there are times when I wonder if our implementation of these ideals fulfills our intentions. Why is it that lay-people cannot interpret our laws themselves? Why are laws written with such convoluted phrasing and obfuscating parlance? Why all the Latin? It seems that beyond the big moral imperatives—no murdering, no stealing, no setting your neighbor's shed ablaze—our laws have grown beyond a mere set of rules to frame our civilization, becoming a maze of switches, levers, and automations that exist to be gamed by a select few who are properly certified or properly financed—the same clans that wrote the rules and continue to contort them. It seems these clans have afforded themselves great job security by crafting our nation's laws in a language that only they understand.

Case in point, consider having a surrogate child in the US in 2008, twenty-two years after the first successful gestational surrogacy in the US happened in 1986. Despite twenty-two years of history, US family law still had no understanding that surrogacy might even exist. Legally speaking, any child born to a gestational surrogate is the child of that surrogate. Further, if the surrogate is married, the child is legally considered to be the offspring of her husband—there is no legal relationship to the biological parents at all. More than a thousand babies were born to gestational surrogates in the US in 2008, and in every case whoever the baby came out of was considered the legal mother by default. After consulting with a specialized (and expensive) lawyer, we were told of a legal workaround: in order to be declared the father, I could file a paternity suit against Rachel's husband, Curtis. If Curtis stipulated to the suit, I would be declared the father of his wife's child. There was no workaround or recourse for Tina; yet another way she was driven outside of her own pregnancy. Tina would have to *adopt her own children* after they were born. It was inconceivably humiliating and unnecessary. Rachel had had a tubal ligation —self-selected to be biologically out of the running for any additional children of her own. We had receipts for thousands of dollars' worth of surrogacy services and multiple doctors and nurses who would have been happy to attest to the implantation. But none of that carried any legal weight. I was left to file a paternity suit against my own brother-in-law, the pastor, over my sister's unborn children. But that was nothing compared to Tina's situation of needing to legally adopt her own flesh and blood. It definitely wasn't good, satisfactory, or even reasonable—I'd say it landed somewhere between absurd and horrifying.

Fortunately, our specialist lawyer had much of the distasteful process streamlined. Forms were mostly boilerplate. Curtis stipulated to the suit, capitulating to the nonsense, and we never had to appear in court in person. That didn't make it less awful: MACDONALD, Mark v. MULDER, Curtis, COURT OF MULTNOMAH COUNTY, OR. It was unseemly. In addition to the paternity suit, there were contracts, waivers, and detailed agreements in place to protect all parties throughout the surrogacy process, legally preventing any of us from backing out halfway through. Signatures, notaries, and couriers; lawyers, clerks, and court fees—all the well-paid trappings of our system. At least, in the end, all the legal i's were dotted and all the t's were crossed—one less thing to fret upon before the birth. We steeled ourselves against the possibility of any unknown errors in our legal preparations, assembled our paperwork into an organized folder, and put our faith in the system, such as it was. Little did we know that the hospital lawyers in North Carolina might refuse to recognize court orders made by Oregon judges when the babies arrived and undo so much of our work, a bitter moment that we can look forward to reading more about in Chapter 35.

I never did get a straight answer from any of the lawyers involved as to why US law couldn't catch up to 21st century medical practices, or why the solution was a series of offensive workarounds instead of changes to the laws themselves. Don't get me wrong, I don't think all lawyers are bad. Vincent would later marry one, and she is lovely. And I really did like our surrogacy lawyer, and I know she did her best for us. Most of all, my own father, whom I love dearly, was a lawyer for many, many years. I believe he is one of the good ones, too—seeking clarity of purpose, easement of grievances, and fairness in society. I have nothing but respect for him and honor what he achieved in his lifetime of hard work. But parts of our legal system clearly remain broken, or at least in dire need of updating. A gestational surrogacy between a family of committed participants ought not to cost thousands of dollars in legal fees, nor should it implicitly question the legitimacy of the biological parents. For the sake of those who came after us, I hope the laws have been updated since 2008—I honestly don't know whether or not they have.

We got past it ourselves and selfishly never looked back. Perhaps that's the flaw in our system right there.

Chapter 32—A Meeting of Mothers (Mark)

Rachel's eldest daughter, Kyra, turned ten in 2008, and to celebrate that milestone, Marilyn offered to take Kyra on a trip to anywhere she liked—just the two of them. It was to be a grandmother/granddaughter adventure. Kyra chose Niagara Falls, and, in mid-June, she and Marilyn took their road trip together. After the Falls, they planned to head up to nearby Toronto to visit Marilyn's family. Marilyn asked me if she could also visit my mother while in Toronto. The request was strange to me. I could not imagine how difficult such a meeting would be for either of them. And I wasn't sure if it would be easier or harder for them without me there, but I was confident that it would be easier on me to not be there, so I said I would enquire. My mother appeared willing so I gave Marilyn the green light. Kyra and Marilyn would stop by my parents' home for lunch on the final day in Toronto. And so, my mother and my biological mother met for the first time over sandwiches in my parents' home, 35 years after my adoption. While they exchanged perspectives on my origin and childhood, I waited nervously in Oregon to hear how it went.

Journal entry, Marilyn, June 27, 2008

Well Mark. I sometimes use pen and paper when I want to think slow. Messy, but more personal.

I'm back from my trip with Kyra. We had a marvelous time. It is "not my grandma's Niagara Falls." Where we had picnics on the grass and the falls of the Niagara River for entertainment. I accomplished what I hoped for and deposited a load of unconditional love into Kyra's soul. Who knows when she'll need to draw on it.

Your directions to your folks were clear—their home was easy to find. Who knew there were neighborhoods like that in downtown Toronto? I stopped at a flower shop nearby and got some fresh flowers—didn't want to arrive empty handed. Kyra wore a big pink flowery hat she had chosen at a kiosk. So we were a strange couple, bedecked with an arm load of flowers and Kyra looking like she had been on a bender. :)

The entranceway and your mom's greeting reminded me of visiting my grandma Iva in downtown Hamilton.

Clearly waiting for us, and curious, we were welcomed warmly, as I knew we would be, from your words. It was strange though. At first, we talked about nothing as if we were distant relatives—but there was an underlying current of electricity between us.

Kyra wanted to know, as we drove to visit them, if they were her grandparents, because, as she reasoned, if they were Uncle Mark's parents, then they were her grandparents. I told her they were her "love grandparents" and we could ask them what she could call them.

This was our first entry into real conversation. They both seemed pleased at the discussion and said we are extended family, which is how I see it. How can we not be family?

(I am such a messy writer—oh well!)

So, she called them Grandma Liz and Grandpa Jim.

We began to talk about our experiences on the opposite ends of the adoption. You would have been interested to have seen their intense interest. I doubt you know (as no kid really knows) how precious you were/are to them. How you have lit up their life and brought a rich sense of joy to them.

I learned some interesting details:

– I knew about them in December, late, but they did not hear about you until February 13—a day your mom says she will never forget.

– The reason that you were six weeks in foster care is that the Social Services doubted that I would go through with the adoption—if they had spent any time with me, they would have been more sure. But since I was young, no parental support, and insisting on seeing, holding you, I was high risk. (It still makes me sad, and angry. I know I was still an adolescent formation and didn't have enough "self" to give, but then I knew that <u>then</u> too.) So many ways to be marginalized!

– I learned that the year your parents adopted Neil there were over 1,200 hospital adoptions in Toronto and the next year it dropped to below 100, due to abortions and girls being encouraged to keep their children.

– That you were considered a "Blue Ribbon" baby. And I think your folks were chosen because of your dad's relationship with Social Services. You got a "<u>Blue Ribbon</u>" home.

The timeline of our meeting you was important to them as you said.

I believe I was able to quell any residual fear/insecurity your mom may have felt. I liked her a lot—her wide smile and open heart.

Your dad is not very self-disclosing, but was engaged with me—told me some stories. At one point I told him (when Liz was in the kitchen) how I felt crazy possessive love for you (immature fifteen-year-old love) when we first met—and how my contemplative meditation helped me "gentle" that down. We were talking about spirituality at the time. He spoke of the Buddhist goal of detachment—attachment being the source of suffering.

I didn't say it, but the center of Christian thinking is that inordinate attachment to stuff and power is a privation of good, but attachment to people in self-giving love, while <u>causing</u> suffering, is the highest good. (For example, what Rachel is doing.)

I enjoyed talking to him—obviously a thinker and lover of ideas.

We had a gracious lunch and they took us to see your home and school.

Mark, this was very good for me. It "thickened" up your life in my mind. I was able to see the layers of experience, formation, community, and interaction you've been given. I "see" you so much better—who you are.

A line from an ancient piece of literature comes to mind. "The lines have fallen to me in pleasant places."

This is indeed true for you, and also for me. With so many wild cards in our deck, our stories could both be so different. So much poorer.

You have been treasured and blessed in ways known to you and hidden from you. I love your family home—multi-layered, interesting, thoughtful. Rich with resources—and flawed because it's peopled with humans.

When we left, your dad didn't say goodbye. He said thank you. I will treasure that.

So we (I) have traversed another mountain range. I really believe it was a gift to your folks as much as to me. Peace has come to replace fear. Friendship has pushed aside competition.

So now I have those values! And see what kind of a family <u>you</u> can build.

I will always love you, as I always have. You are in my heart where I hold gently the gifts of my life.

Marilyn (who was with you at the beginning)

Chapter 33—Distractions (Mark)

About five weeks prior to the birth, there were no major issues or crises. Things were progressing smoothly and according to plan. At home we were shopping, painting, and planning. Getting everything ready. Crossing as much off the To-Do list as possible. There were cribs to assemble, clothes and diapers to buy, and the sometimes-overwhelming idea of real, actual children living in our home to wrap our heads around. Along with eager anticipation, anxiety was growing steadily for me, but I did my best to pack the anxiety away somewhere deep inside and ignore it. One of my boxes to check was a routine follow-up with my dermatologist—the eczema rash that had brought me to him a few months prior now long since cleared up.

The appointment started unremarkably, an ordinary check-up, every inch of my arm closely inspected with bright lights and a magnifying glass. Everything was fine—eczema gone—as I had expected, having not seen any signs myself in weeks. We were wrapping up when I had an afterthought:

"Hey Doc," I asked, "this is unrelated to the rash, but could you recommend a good lotion? I have this little patch of dry skin on my temple that is being a bit stubborn."

"Hmm, let me take a quick look," and he peered at the side of my head for only a brief moment. "Ah, yeah, that's not a dry spot," he said matter-of-factly. "What you've got there is a basal cell carcinoma."

Wait, that's cancer. Carcinoma means cancer. Isn't carcinoma cancer? I blurted, "Um, okay, so what does that mean? Does that mean I have cancer?"

The doctor confidently explained that everything would be fine. The calmness in his voice competed with the queasiness in my stomach for my attention. He called basal cell "the turtles of all cancers," and said that if I had to get any type of cancer, this was the one to have and it did not look to have spread too far yet. Essentially, all we needed to do was cut it out. I sat numbly through his explanations and absorbed what I could. My carefully packed and secured bundle of anxieties was smashed like Wile E. Coyote hitting a painting of a tunnel on a cliff face.

I have never done particularly well when it comes to managing worry. I can worry with the best of them. I often worry when there is nothing to worry about. Always a little tense, quick to pace and fret. I suspect that my habits of planning and calculating are, to some extent, coping mechanisms to help me deal with everyday anxiety. I would eventually learn that anxiety is a known ripple in the Elliott gene pool, and talking with them about it—comparing notes and strategies—would greatly assist me with the coping. But for now, I felt alone. It was only the surety of the doctor's words and the unambiguous science behind the upbeat prognosis that helped me find my footing.

There is a procedure called Mohs surgery that has an extremely high success rate in removing this particular type of cancer. There was nothing for me to worry about—the procedure was common and there was no reason to think that my situation wouldn't be handled easily. It would just be a few days to confirm the diagnosis with a biopsy and then they would schedule the Mohs right away.

Nine days later I walked through the automatic sliding glass door of an outpatient Mohs surgery clinic in Tualatin, OR, and found myself in what appeared to be the nurse's office of a particularly violent retirement home. There were four or five elderly folks sitting about the room with gauze taped to their noses, necks, or arms, some with others sitting next to them, quietly supportive. They all waited patiently in the solid, upright chairs and were perhaps comforted by the muted colors that surrounded them. Those who had companions with them sat quietly with no more than an occasional murmur of consultation. Those who didn't sat in silence by themselves. An older television set played CNN in one corner, volume low enough that the voices were indiscernible, but loud enough to prevent the deafening silences that form so easily in such places. Tina had to be at work that day, so I was one of the loners, and was glad for the radiant glow of the television with its silently scrolling tickertape of the day's news.

Mohs surgery is a remarkable thing. As I understand it, they excise a single patch of cancerous skin and then immediately scan its edges for cancer cells. If the edges are clear, then they must have removed all the cancer; if they find cancerous cells on a border of the removed skin, then there are still cancer cells in the patient too, and they take another pass. The success rate for Mohs surgery on basal cell carcinoma is something like 98% or better—pretty good odds. I mentally gave thanks to Dr. Fredric Mohs, may he rest in peace, as I sat, thankful that this particular trauma came with a pre-calculated, follow-directions-on-the-box solution. There were no options for me to weigh, no planning required, no extra balls for me to add to the cascade I was already struggling to keep aloft. It was also comforting that this quiet clinic was such a well-oiled Mohs surgery machine. They did dozens of these procedures every day, five patients at a time rotating in and out of two surgical rooms. Cut, sit, test, wait; cut, sit, test, wait. When your sample came back clean, they stitched you up and sent you home. They knew exactly what they were doing. If I could muster the patience to get through this, the cancer would just be another checked box on my To-Do list that I could get past.

After I checked in at the reception, I took my place in the rotation. As I merged into the roundabout of treatments, I realized that the gauze bandages that adorned the various patches of skin on my fellow waiting-room inmates was essentially covering open wounds—surgeries-in-progress, not scrapes from playground scuffles. No wonder there wasn't much conversation in the room. I saw the doctor five times that day, no more than fifteen minutes per session. A quick briefing and analgesic, three passes with the scalpel, and then twenty-seven swift and precise stitches and I was done. As I merged out of the roundabout, I nodded to the other travelers that I had been silently swapping seats with for the past three hours and went home, frankly none the worse for wear.

It was, strangely, the best and worst time to get cancer. At month eight of the pregnancy, I was far too busy preparing, planning, fretting, and marshaling my courage to worry about anything new. On the other hand, I was far too busy preparing, planning, fretting, and marshaling my courage to worry about anything new. At this point my sanity hung by a tenuous thread. I pressed forward, at times mechanically, in the hopes that someday soon I would emerge from the other side with two children and nothing but a small scar to remind me of the time I visited the Mohs factory.

Ten days later, on a Friday morning, a competent nurse at the clinic removed my stitches and that same afternoon I headed to the airport with Tina, flying to North Carolina to await the birth. Over the next few days everyone would be assembling together there—Tina and I; Rachel and Curtis; Liz and Jim; Marilyn and Steve; and Irma and Kolf (Tina's parents). Even Vincent was scheduled to make an appearance. The transition from carcinoma to Carolina was either the sublime to the ridiculous or the ridiculous to the sublime.

Tina and I had rented a house in Raleigh with several extra rooms to help accommodate everyone, and there were many comings and goings. But like a couple before their wedding, we were excused from many of the casual goings-on. Clearly, some of those goings-on would be less casual than others—my biological father meeting my parents for the first time, for example—but I remained too distracted and too stressed to notice, and let those events proceed on their own.

There are burdens that come with being adopted. One of them is balancing the love for your parents and the respect for your biological roots—whether those roots are known or unknown. I suspect that the mere idea of these two worlds meeting would quicken the heart of any adopted person. It is hard to convey the root of that fear. It is like a distilled version of your spouse meeting your ex. There are deep feelings, an unchangeable history, and an undercurrent of unfounded guilt for some reason that I don't understand. Regardless, it feels like no good can come from such a meeting. It is a delicate and perilous thing, paradoxical and subtly heartbreaking at its core. It cannot help but disappoint someone. For me, this meeting coincided with the birth of Aly and Zoe and, like the first meeting of Marilyn and my parents, I more-or-less missed it. Small mercies.

Of course, there were parts of this first encounter for which I was present. I do remember that there was a dinner out. I remember my father, the recently converted Zen-Buddhist, asking both Steve and Curtis about their beliefs in God, leading to a vigorous discussion about whether He really even existed. I remember my mother puttering around with Marilyn in the kitchen of the rented home—comparing and contrasting everything with competitive zeal. It was cordial and outwardly affectionate, but I sensed some measure of deep-seated rivalry. In my preoccupation, I could not see the depths of it. In a way, it felt like I wasn't there, or was watching it happen on TV. I didn't have the strength to be more present than that. In any other circumstances, these meetings would have dominated my conscious mind. But not that week. I sincerely hope everything went okay.

Chapter 34—The Birth (Rachel)

It's very early, and I am not a morning person. Despite this, I shower, because who knows when I will have the chance to shower again, and then gather up my toiletries into a bag. I'll be sleeping at the hospital tonight.

The four of us, Mark, Tina, Curtis, and I, gather around the nurses' station. "We're here for a scheduled C-section," I say. There are clearly too many of us, and a brief look of confusion flutters across the woman's face before it clicks, *The Surrogacy*. The staff has been brought up to date and prepared in advance of our arrival. Special dispensations were made to allow for everyone to be in the surgical suite. It was a bit of a battle, but Mark & Tina needed to see their daughters born; I needed my husband to support me; and none of us would back down. It was just not a fight the hospital was going to win. Nodding to herself, the nurse comes around the U-shaped desk, and as the obviously pregnant one, I am separated from my herd and taken to a curtained-off little room to undress and lie down. We'll be reunited soon, I am assured.

I'm alone in a white room, wearing a faded blue gown and lying on the scratchy hospital blanket. Cold and nerves have made me chilly, and I wait for someone to come by who can get me an extra blanket. The first person is no help at all, a phlebotomist who inserts my IV. I think to myself, "Good. Drugs." The second person, also without access to a blanket, is the anesthesiologist who is there to walk me through the process of the spinal block. *Like an epidural, but stronger.* None of the good drugs for me until after the birth, because even at this late stage the little lives inside of me could be affected. He's right, of course. I don't want that. But I'm freezing now, and I don't know where Curtis or Mark are. I'm starting to feel nervous. I'm lonely.

A nurse! A kind and cheerful face, and most importantly, she has access to blankets, even hot ones. She layers me up with steaming blankets, tenderly tucking them in, around and under my feet before checking my vitals and telling me, "The doctor will be here soon." I'm assuming this means the doctor is still in bed.

As she turns to go, a face slips around the edge of the curtain. My mom. She is beaming, almost crying. "Oh, Rae!"

I don't mean this to sound heartless, but she is not the one I want to see. She needs more from me than I can give right now. I'm overwhelmed, truly overwhelmed, for the first time since this whole thing started. I really just want to see Curtis. But here Mom is, having talked her way past the guards to tell me that the parents—all six of them—and The Girls are going to Elmer's for breakfast. They'll be back in plenty of time, I am promised. A quick kiss and she's gone, and I'm alone again. Why did they need me here so early? I have no idea. I feel like I've been lying here for hours.

Finally, the people I need show up. Mark, Tina, and Curtis. We are a team, the four of us. In it together. Their smiles relieve me, even though I can see they are as nervous as I am. I wonder if Curtis is worried about me, worried about the surgery? Should I be worried? Surely not. Surely this happens every day?

The four of us smile at each other foolishly. This is it. We made it. There are memories of the last nine months bandied back and forth, stories remembered and shared.

Curtis holds my hand and kisses my forehead. Having them all there soothes me.

Here is the nurse again, this time bearing not blankets, but head-to-toe surgical gear for the three of them. If they're going in, they're going to be suited and booted. I laugh at them in their paper hats and masks and wonder aloud why I don't need to wear all that stuff.

"Because you are already exposed to all of your own germs, dear," says the nurse, who is now unlocking the wheels of the bed. She navigates me around the white curtain and Curtis, Tina, and Mark follow behind us. When we get to the surgical suite there is a small kerfuffle when one of the staff says that we can't all possibly go in, but we set him straight. Vigorously. There is no way in hell any of us is getting left behind.

It's funny. They don't give me any of the good drugs, but I feel weird. Fuzzy. It's probably my brain releasing serious chemicals to help me cope as I struggle to bend forward enough and hold still enough for the anesthesiologist to slip the needle between my vertebrae. My legs are hilariously rubbery. I can't feel them or move them, though I do try. I feel oddly disconnected from my own body, even more so after they drape and hang the curtain between my chest and the rest of my body. My team is circled around my head, stroking my hair, hand on my shoulder. Curtis is on a stool, but I think Mark and Tina are standing. It's hard to tell, really, but they will need a clear view of the babies while Curtis only needs to see me, so I'm pretty sure.

I feel odd sensations, but not pain or anything even close, when the doctor begins her incision. I wonder if Mark and Tina can see it. I wonder if they are looking into my body. I know Curtis isn't. He wouldn't be able to cope. Then suddenly a feeling of partial physical relief and a

187

crying, purple little person is held above the curtain. For the life of me, all I can think of is *The Lion King*. It's just like that.

"It's a girl! She's perfect."

And she is whisked to the incubator standing by. Mark hesitates, I can feel him, but I tell him to go be with his daughter. I know he doesn't want to abandon me, but he is already a father and his first allegiance should be to someone on the other side of the room. He and Tina go, and quickly the rest of the pressure in my abdomen abates and another little miracle is held above the curtain for me to see, another perfect girl. Into a second incubator. Six pounds, seven ounces and six pounds, six ounces of pure love, swaddled and crying and perfect.

I close my eyes and it hurts more to be put back together than it did to be taken apart. I think maybe Curtis is crying, but I'm too tired to check. We did it. I did it. I can't believe it. And it's done.

Chapter 35—Welcome (Mark)

On August 19th, 2008, the twins were born in Durham, North Carolina. Incredibly, it was precisely one year to the day from the evening that Rachel offered to be our surrogate over dinner in our Oregon dining room. Sometimes life happens more quickly than we expect.

Tina, Curtis, and I, all dressed in sterile bunny suits and hats, were at Rachel's side when first Zoe Rachel and then a moment later Alaska Rachel came into this world. Tina and I had decided many weeks prior that both girls would carry the middle name Rachel in honor of their aunt and all she had given to allow them to be. The birth was a planned caesarian and was completed without incident. Our girls were normal, healthy little six-and-a-half-pound gifts, foisted upon our inexperience and immediately embraced as the beloved nexus of our family. Tina and I took Zoe and Aly to the generously sized room which we had been assigned. Rachel was taken to a recovery room in another part of the maternity ward. Parents, nieces, siblings, and more parents flitted back and forth. Everyone was there. Our room was boisterous and full of genuine happiness. Too much posing for pictures and too little sleep were overpowered by a grand sense of accomplishment. The girls' first breaths reminded us of the wonders of life; renewing within each of us, in different ways, feelings of hope and optimism. For Tina and me, those first breaths transformed our marriage into a family. Sadly, the keen eyes of the law failed to recognize that transformation.

Astonishingly, we were told by the staff at the hospital that this was the first gestational surrogacy that they had ever handled. This was a huge university hospital with an international reputation, how could we possibly be their first? Initially, we assumed it would be nothing more than an interesting footnote to our saga. From the doctor's perspective there were no issues, for them it was like any other birth—but the nurses and support staff struggled to adjust to multiple parents, too many grandparents and other interested onlookers that were not part of the norm. They struggled with room assignments and visitor permissions. More seriously, somewhere in the back offices of the hospital, the lawyers were particularly vexed. They clamped down on our delight, deciding that they could not accept any of our carefully planned and executed court orders or adoption papers because they were from out-of-state. Without discussion or consent, they registered Rachel's and Curtis's names on the twins' birth certificates and social security records. In the eyes of the law, or at least the eyes of the hospital's legal office, my family belonged to someone else.

There are times when bureaucracy can be cold, callous even, but this felt almost intentionally cruel. My heart's defenses had been laid bare by all that had happened in the weeks leading up to that day, and the stab from lawyers' blade drove deeply into my chest. I am proud to say that rather than crumpling before them, the sharp pain gave me focus and purpose. I stood up to them with uncharacteristic vehemence, even though I know my protestations affected little. I was ill-equipped for this battle and utterly impotent against their procedural battlements. To this day, I still harbor serious bitterness that I will never get back the time I spent on the phone yelling at lawyers on the morning my daughters were born. When I should have been holding my babies, I was instead debating rules and legal standings with obstinate attorneys. My circumstances were overwhelming enough without this added bullshit—my twins had just been birthed from my long-lost sister, two and half thousand miles from home; I had just been diagnosed and cured of cancer; and my parents and my biological parents had just met for the first time. The last thing I should have been doing that morning was standing in the corner, arguing minutia with mule-headed strangers who lacked the courage to stray from their uncaring scripts when the right thing to do was so simple and so obvious. Throughout much of the day of the birth, and many of those that followed, the festering legal wranglings kept dragging me away from precious time with my new family. It took a concerted effort to stay in the loveliness of those first moments with my girls.

But the important news was that the girls were born. They were loved. They were safe. The miracle had happened. They were ours (or would be, damn it). They were ours to raise, ours to love, ours to encourage, discipline, and mentor. Zoe and Aly were at the beginning of their journey. In exchange for making us a family, Tina and I would devote our lives to giving them the best possible start in this world that we could.

Despite the delight brought by the arrival of the girls, chaos seemed to find a way to follow us, even after we escaped the hospital and returned to the rental house. I should have been able to start to relax, I thought. After all, we had gotten through the most difficult part and our house was filled with so many supportive and loving people. Friends of Rachel's brought us meals and flowers. Grandparents cleaned, fed, and generally kept everything else going for us. Still, I found myself unable to unwind. I wanted nothing more than for everything to be over, for our new family to be back in Oregon. Often, when the stress got too much for me, I would retreat to our rented bedroom, clinging to my rationality with all the resolution I could muster. Scintillations invaded my field of vision causing the sunlit blinds to dance and shimmer in time with my anxiety. I would do my best to fight back, forcing myself to take deeper breaths and trying to ground myself to something. Anything.

I was buried in one of those moments of panicky retreat on the second day back in the house when I heard Tina's awful call to me from outside, "Mark! Call 911!"

All over my body, my skin suddenly tightened and prickled painfully—immediately erupting in a cold sweat, again. I could hear a ringing in my ears. As I bolted to attention, my life flashed before my eyes, or rather, the girls' not-yet-realized lives did.

"Mark! Call 911. My dad fell in the driveway."

I swayed to my feet, stomach churning, limbs robotically carrying me down the stairs as fast as they could. My mind tried to recover; at least it was not about the girls, I don't know if I could have survived that. In shock, I called 911 for the first time in my life as I nearly tumbled down the stairs. I gave what information I could to the calming voice on the other end of the line. Help would be on the way soon. I met Tina at the doorway and she breathlessly relayed the details. Her father had fallen on the steep driveway taking out the recycling cart and cracked his head pretty badly on the concrete. He had been suffering for some time with an affliction that diminished his capacity and affected his balance, but he would not be stopped from contributing to the household. I felt a deep pang of sympathy for the man, but instead of heading outside to join the others helping him, I turned to the living room and went to secure the girls, leaving Tina and her mom to deal with the ambulance crew that arrived shortly thereafter.

Within a few days, Tina's dad seemed okay, or at least as okay as he was before the fall. There were plenty of spare hands to help take care of him as well. Family leans in when things like this happen and we all pitched in with whatever we had left in the tank. Exhaustion be damned.

The doctors had told us not to fly with infants less than ten days old, and so on the eleventh day we left for home. The girls were both doing well and settling into a routine by then, but I worried about airport check in and security. In North Carolina they were legally still Rachel and Curtis's children. Could we be charged with kidnapping our own children? At this point nothing would surprise me. Fortunately, it was worry for naught, as the airline never even asked for their IDs. Actually, the whole travel experience went remarkably well. The girls were too small to make much noise and were so adorably new that everyone wanted to peak at them and to lend us a hand. After we made it home safely, we followed our lawyer's guidance and appealed directly to the State of North Carolina to get the proper names on our daughters' documents and have the birth certificates reissued. They were reasonable and accepted our Oregon court documents without question, although the process took several weeks, another course of paperwork, and naturally another round of fees. During the interim, we had an interesting success: an Oregon court certified in a precedent-setting ruling that Tina was the biological mother of the girls, despite their being carried by Rachel, and so Tina avoided having to legally adopt her own children after all. Small mercies.

Most importantly, our family was home.

Part 3—Family

Chapter 36—Reflections on Surrogacy (Rachel)

It's hard to reconcile all the years that have passed with the immediacy of all the memories of the year they were created. Time seems at once to be flying by and standing still.

From my "Auntie Rachel" point of view, I would say that Zoe looks like our side of the family, with a grin that I worry might bust her face in half, but is more like her mom in nature. She tends to the introverted side but has a sneaky sense of humor that belies her quiet nature. Aly favors her mom—a little darker, a little slighter—but is more like her dad. The wonders of biology! She is a whirling dervish of a girl, all personality and sass. They are both too smart for their own good, or mine for that matter, but being raised by parents with intelligence and intention will do that, I suppose.

There is a day that stands out in my mind, several years ago, when I was visiting them in Oregon. We were walking the dog, or at the zoo (I can't remember), and the sky was so, so blue. In the spirit of the kind of mom I am, I pointed it out and wondered aloud to the girls what made the sky blue. In unison, their little mop-heads swiveled to look at me and Aly said on behalf of both of them, in a vaguely disdainful voice, "It's called Rayleigh scattering, Auntie Rachel." They couldn't have been more than four or five. And that's how I learned what Rayleigh scattering is.

They are stuck at that age in my head, although I know those days are long gone. The sense of sheer *aliveness* that vibrates off of them is intoxicating to me. A better writer could capture the sparks that fly from their eyes and the joy with which they interact with the world. My words are too small to do them justice.

Sometimes I forget that I did this. There are periods of time that pass where the crazy, insane eighteen months described in these pages lie dormant in my heart, unthought-of and a little dusty with time. Inevitably though, a conversation arises, or a memory is triggered, and suddenly I remember: I did that! Who knew I was that kind of person? I didn't.

People usually shake their heads and say that I gave Mark and Tina an incredible gift, and on one hand I know that's true. But the reverse is also true. During those months, I received an incredible gift of my own—the gift of my big brother. You can't completely make up for thirty-one years of not knowing one another, but we came as close as it's possible, I think. In a remarkably short time, Mark went from my "secret" brother, to my "new" brother, to just my brother. Someone I can talk to, count on, make fun of, ignore, enjoy, and disagree with—but most of all, someone I love. Who loves me right back. The night I sat down and wrote my first email to him, I never imagined that it could be like this; that *we* would be like this. Just Family. That is my gift, and I will be grateful for it until my last breath.

Chapter 37—Family (Mark)

Years have passed and the twins are growing up. The story of our nuclear family is receding comfortably into normalcy. Our journey is now the journey of every family—bumps and bruises, bedtime stories, school days, snow days, pets, best friends, and braces. We all know that part of the journey, so I won't dwell on it here. I will confirm that raising twins is not always easy and we have been grateful to have the love and support of three sets of grandparents; Marilyn and Steve settled naturally into the role of "third" grandparents and the girls don't really differentiate between their relationship with them and their relationship with my parents or Tina's parents. Their position as grandparents has also been good for my own relationship with Marilyn and Steve. The girls give us a common purpose and a familiar social context that eases things tremendously. Consider Marilyn trying to find an appropriate Christmas gift for the son she gave up for adoption and did not see again for thirty-five years: an impossibly delicate task. A task with no right answer. But spoiling grandchildren comes easily and gives us both a safe, neutral territory of shared love and no regrets.

It makes me happy to see how the girls act as salve for Marilyn's sense of loss, both in their very existence and as a reflection of the loving acts of her own daughter that helped create them.

Several years after the girls were born, Tina and I decided that it was time for me to get a vasectomy. It was an easy decision, more of an admission of age than anything else, and I soon found myself in another doctor's office. The waiting room was again the typical combination of warm tones, well-thumbed magazines, and padded chairs with bare wooden arms. Do all doctors share the same decorator? Perhaps it is something they study in medical school: Soothing Beige Colors 101.

Twenty minutes after I arrived, my name was called and a nurse led me to a small clinic room. He asked me to undress and put on the light cotton hospital gown that had been laid out for me. Seven uncomfortable, half-naked minutes passed before the doctor came in and introduced herself. She perched on a swivel stool and held a folder of my paperwork in one hand and gold-trimmed ballpoint pen in the other. I sat fidgeting on the paper-covered exam table in my poorly secured gown as she explained the details of the procedure.

After outlining the various steps and recovery instructions, being medically accurate without being excessively graphic, she asked the obligatory and expected question, "So, are you completely sure that you don't want to have any more kids?"

In the brief moment it took me to consider the question, a cavalcade of thoughts and memories flooded through me, each overlapping and cutting one another off, similar to the way your life can flash before your eyes in a moment of dire fear, but without the fear. It was an easy but complicated answer . . .

I thought about Aly and Zoe and how much they had grown since the birth. Rambunctious girls now, they were happy, healthy, smart, and curious. Amazingly, Aly, the fetus that had always been wriggling, stretched out across the top in the ultrasounds, continues to be the more active one of the twins in many ways and is interested in everything (except perhaps humility). Zoe, the calm fetus, has great powers of focus and concentration that have helped her to excel in math and arts. The girls have become the center of our world and our lives continue to shift around them. Like all parents, we have realigned our schedules, priorities, dreams, and savings to their needs. For the last few years, I have also substantially reduced my work hours—choosing the life side of the work/life balance—happy to have the opportunity to trade some measure of financial security for more time with them.

I thought about Rachel and how wonderful it was to have the surrogacy to bring us together. It broke down walls and created new resilient bonds that would last forever. In those first two years we knew one another, we went through a lifetime of trials, joys, pains, and laughter. We are as close and comfortable with each other now as any siblings might be—confidants, look-outs, and companions. No matter the passage of time apart, we fall back into easy, intimate conversation in less time than it takes to pour a glass of wine.

I thought about the other two of the four healthy, fertilized ova that the doctors created from our genetic material—the ones that were put into cold storage at the time of the IVF implantation. A year after the girls were born, a letter had arrived from the fertility clinic because it was time to decide the fate of those remaining eggs. We were offered three options: they could be implanted as a second surrogacy; they could be scrapped; or they could be donated to stem cell research. The eggs were not children, they were just samples of viable genetic material in a freezer in a lab somewhere, but I knew that they had the potential to grow into something wonderful. Maybe they could have become the boys to complement our girls? But a second surrogacy was an impossibility, a greedy indulgence of which we wouldn't be capable. We were spent and, more importantly, we were sated. Tina and I wrestled only briefly with the sad decision that had to be made. Our path was clear. Ever the pragmatists, Tina and I would opt for the donation to research. Some weeks later, the frozen eggs were shipped to Harvard where they would be used to support stem cell research activities. Hopefully some good will come from our small sacrifice. I suppose it is possible that one day the work there could find a cure for the kidney disease that afflicts Tina and millions of others.

I thought about my own adoption and all the questions that began this story, all my questions about connectedness. Then I thought about my reconnection with Marilyn, my birth mother, and about my developing relationships with my other new siblings, Vincent and Benjamin. I thought about my parents, Jim and Liz, that raised me and helped make me what I am today. I thought about my biological place in the world, which seemed more tangible now than ever before—both its past, its present, and, with addition of the girls, its future. And I thought about all the remarkable events, all the seeming impossibilities that needed to happen to make our story possible. The girls were the result of a confluence of miracles; circumstances that could never be replicated. They were a gift, or more accurately, a reward. We had spent more than a decade planning, searching, hoping, spending, finding, loving, and sacrificing to bring them into our lives. The gift is what Rachel did for Tina and me, and for the girls. It was a gift we can never repay. But the girls themselves are a hard-fought reward for our perseverance as a family. All of us. We *earned* them. This is my family.

A small smile crept across my face as I replied to the doctor with simply, "Oh no, we're definitely finished."

Perhaps the smile came across as glib or callous because the doctor paused and looked at me, lowering her folder slightly. I don't expect she gets many grins in response to that particular question. For a brief moment, I considered telling her the whole story behind my smile, a rich and lengthy story of hope and love and satisfaction. This story. But we had work to get done and this was not the time. Doctor, I thought as she looked at me, you have no idea what it took to create the kids we have. The twins will be plenty, thank you. I'll wait patiently and happily for grandkids someday, but for now, my family is complete.

"All right then," she replied, "let's get on with it."

About the Authors

Rachel Elliott is a native Canadian who migrated south (like the geese) to escape the cold. She lives in North Carolina with her husband, Brent, and dog, Swagger, and is a proud mom to two grown daughters. She would rather be at the beach than anywhere else and loves to find an adventure. An avid reader, and recreational writer, this is her first published work.

Mark MacDonald lives in Beaverton, Oregon with his wife of twenty-one years, Tina, their two children, Zoe and Alaska, and seemingly countless pets. His day jobs are engineering technology development and education. He is an unabashed science nerd and an avid supporter of women in STEM fields. An author of numerous academic publications and patents, this is his first popular non-fiction work.

About the Press

Unsolicited Press was founded in 2012 and is based out of Portland, Oregon. Many of its authors are award-winning and champions in their respective genres. The team works hard to publish voices that tackle difficult topics and bravely wade into the experimental. Learn more at unsolicitedpress.com.